GW01003509

Manage
Your Time

Manage
Your Time

Control your
workload and make
time for success

JAMES MANKTELOW

**LONDON, NEW YORK,
MUNICH, MELBOURNE, DELHI**

Project Editor	Tom Broder
Project Art Editor	Edward Kinsey
Senior Editor	Simon Tuite
Senior Art Editor	Sara Robin
Assistant Editors	Amber Tokeley
	Tarda Davison-Aitkins
Assistant Designer	Kathryn Wilding
DTP Designer	Traci Salter
Production Controller	Elizabeth Cherry
Picture Researcher	Sarah Hopper
Special Photography	Roger Dixon
Executive Managing Editor	Adèle Hayward
Managing Art Editor	Karla Jennings
Art Director	Peter Luff
Publisher	Corinne Roberts

First published in 2006 by Dorling Kindersley Limited
80 Strand, London WC2R 0RL
A Penguin Company

2 4 6 8 10 9 7 5 3 1

A CIP catalogue record for this book is
available from the British Library
ISBN-13: 9-7814-0531-288-2
ISBN-10: 1-4053-1288-2

ED244
Printed and bound in China by Leo Paper Group

Contents

Introduction

Time management techniques are some of the most important skills that you can learn. Effective time management will help you to boost your productivity, achieve a more successful and fulfilling career, and get the most out of your personal life.

On one level, the techniques required for good time management can seem quite mundane: they consist of the many small disciplines that successful people use to work more efficiently and more effectively. Viewed in this way, it can seem a dull and unglamorous subject. However, viewed on another level, the techniques you will learn in this book deal with many of the really big questions you will face in life. For example, the time management technique of "goal setting" asks you to think about the ideas, people, and things

 that have real meaning for you in your life. Once you know what's important, time management gives you the tools you need to organize and motivate yourself to turn these most dearly-held dreams into reality.

By learning the time management skills associated with workload management, you will learn how to overcome much of the debilitating stress that drags so many people down. These same skills create the "space" you need for the other things that are important to you – like being a good parent, or starting that business you've always dreamed about. These are the things, so easily crowded out, that bring lasting happiness and fulfillment.

> **Good time management moves you from being active to being effective**

By learning the self-organization and personal effectiveness techniques within this book, you can finally overcome the internal blocks that may be holding you back, and you will develop the laser-sharp focus you need to achieve truly great things. By developing and applying effective delegation and leverage skills, you will be able to reinforce your own efforts with those of other people, and use your intelligence to get truly enormous returns from your time and effort.

So spend a little time with this book. Apply its lessons. Learn to use your time intelligently and creatively. Your small investment of time will be repaid many times over.

Assessing your Skills

The aim of this questionnaire is to get you to think about your everyday time management and assess your scope for improvement – so answer honestly. Complete it before you read the book, choosing the answer that comes closest to your preferred response and putting the appropriate letter in the "Before" box. After you have read the book and applied the techniques, complete the questionnaire again.

	Before	After

1 You feel in control of your workload: **Before:** B
- **A** Rarely.
- **B** Life can be unpredictable, but you usually cope.
- **C** Your schedule is flexible enough to adapt quickly to unexpected events.

2 Your attitude to deadlines is that: **Before:** B
- **A** There's so much to do that sometimes deadlines just have to slip.
- **B** If you can't meet a deadline, you try to alert people in advance.
- **C** You usually deliver good quality work on, or ahead of schedule.

3 When you need to start on a difficult job:
- **A** You have real problems getting going.
- **B** You do it at the last minute.
- **C** You know how to get going, and you start as soon as you can.

4 You've just completed the day's To-Do list: **Before:** B
- **A** What's a To-Do List?
- **B** Good – it's great when it happens.
- **C** You use more powerful time-management tools than To-Do lists.

	Before	After

5 **You chose your career because:**

A You needed the money.
B It seemed interesting.
C You're doing something that really matters to yourself and other people.

Before: A

6 **Your approach to work can best be described as:**

A You do work as it turns up.
B You plan ahead, but events are unpredictable.
C You have a clear view of what you want to achieve, and why you want to achieve it.

Before: A

7 **How would you describe your "work/life balance"?**

A You often work late, and when you leave you worry about things you haven't done.
B You cope, but only by juggling frantically.
C You have time for the things that are important.

Before: B

8 **Your boss asks you to finish an urgent job by lunchtime tomorrow:**

A There's no way you can squeeze this in as well.
B You'll do it somehow.
C You just need to tweak your schedule a bit.

Before: B

9 **When you need to find an important document:**

A You have to shuffle through stacks of paper.
B You can find it quite quickly – sometimes.
C You know exactly where to find it.

Before: B

10 **Frequent interruptions undermine your ability to do your job:**

A You often end the day feeling you've achieved little.
B You accept the need for interruptions, but minimize unnecessary ones.
C Not really – you make time in your schedule for the people who need you, and you meet regularly to deal with issues before they become urgent.

Before: B

Before | After

11 When you're faced with an unusual and difficult task:

A You put off dealing with it until the last minute.
B You're happiest keeping it under your control.
C You prefer to outsource it to an expert.

12 How well do you think you do your work?

A You do everything to the very best of your ability.
B You try to do everything well.
C You do each task as well as it needs to be done.

13 You are doing your next task because:

A You have to do it for an impending meeting.
B It's one of the jobs in your job description.
C It helps you to achieve a major goal.

14 You get help from other people:

A Rarely – you usually have to do it yourself.
B Sometimes, but you're often disappointed by the poor quality of work you get back.
C Often, and you explain jobs carefully when you allocate them, so you're rarely disappointed.

15 People often come to you with problems:

A You feel ground down by the number of people who need your help.
B You coach people in solving their problems.
C You insist people come to you only if they have a considered proposal for solving the problem.

Final Scores

	A	B	C
Before	3	10	10
After			

Analysis
Mostly As

Your answers suggest that you feel out of control of your workload
and of the things being asked of you. However, they also show that
you have a fantastic opportunity to improve the quality of your life,
improve your outcomes and, ultimately, become more successful.
Work through this book in detail, paying particular attention to
the areas where you feel most uncomfortable, and take time to learn
and apply the lessons within it. You will be amazed by the difference.

Mostly Bs

Your answers show an understanding of some of the ideas which lie
behind time management, but they also show that this understanding
does not necessarily translate into settled high-performance habits.
Work through this book, paying particular attention to the areas
where you feel most uncomfortable, and incorporate the techniques
and tips into your working life.

Mostly Cs

You obviously take a focused and well-organized approach to your
working life. You know where you are going, you're broadly in control
of your workload, and you are rarely caught out by unexpected
events. Work through this book, using the various tips and techniques
to move up to the next level. In particular, make sure that you are
"doing the right things" as well as just "doing things right". Pay
particular attention to the chapter on leverage – this will help to bring
you to peak performance.

Conclusion

If this is the first time you have done this self-assessment, then bear in
mind what you have learned from it. Make sure that you pay special
attention to the areas of weakness you have identified, and that you
incorporate the tips and techniques into your everyday working life.
After you have read the book and had an opportunity to put these
techniques into practice, take this quiz again. You should find that
you are not only in full control of your workload, but that you are also
much more effective and much happier.

Know What You Want

1

Time management is not about managing time itself; it is about managing how you use your time. To do this, you need to prioritize the multitude of tasks that confront you, so that you can focus your time and energy on tasks that are important. To help you assess your priorities and work out what you want from life, this chapter shows you how to:

- Understand the importance of creating a "Big Picture" of your life, and of setting life goals
- Formulate your "Plan 60" – a statement of where you would like to be at the age of 60, or some other fixed point in the future
- Create a realistic five-year plan to help you to focus on your short-term goals
- Identify and commit to your top life goals.

Prioritize Your Time

Prioritization is the key to time management. It propels us from reaction mode to action mode, and helps us to avoid wasting valuable time on less important choices.

Use Time Effectively

Time is an extremely valuable commodity, and is one that is perpetually in short supply. In both our professional and personal lives, most of us are confronted with a daily barrage of tasks, and we usually spread ourselves too thin trying to accomplish them all. As a result, we often fail to accomplish any of them effectively. Since we cannot increase the supply of time, all we can do is manage the demand. This is the basic principle underlying effective time management.

> **The setting of priorities is the key to winning back control of your time**

Set Your Priorities

The starting point for effective time management is to set priorities. Everyday we face a mind-boggling array of choices competing for our time and attention. If we do not decide what is important to us (and what is not), we will squander valuable time. On the face of it, prioritization seems like a simple enough exercise. Don't we know what is important to us? Won't we automatically focus on it? Surprisingly enough, the answer to both these questions is often "no". For most of us, life is full of a million-and-one things to do, and it is easy to lose perspective. We have no easy way of deciding between one thing and the next because it all seems equally important and urgent.

> **Urgency engulfs the manager, yet the most urgent task is not always the most important. The tyranny of the urgent lies in its distortion of priorities.**
>
> R. Alec Mackenzie

Pinpoint Your Goals

When we are burdened by an impossible number of tasks and struggling to stay afloat, most of us find it increasingly difficult to distinguish between urgent and important. We allow ourselves to be tyrannized by short-term urgencies, and miss what is really important to our long-term growth and development. It is almost impossible to feel satisfied in such a situation, because we can never catch up with everything on the To-Do list. Driven by urgency, we end each day exhausted, depleted, and dissatisfied, feeling that we didn't do enough. Even if we did get a lot done, there is no real sense of achievement, because we feel overwhelmed by all those tasks that have yet to be done.

Pinpointing goals, rather than urgencies, offers a way out of this trap. Goals help you to both identify and focus on your priorities so that you can evaluate what needs to be done and concentrate your efforts on what really matters to you.

Recognizing Priorities Refusing to be tyrannized by short-term urgencies allows us to focus on those things – such as family and relationships – most important for our long-term development.

Develop Your Big Picture

So that you can rise above the chaos of your daily activities and work out your priorities, you first need to assess what you really want from your life.

Identify Personal Desires

The next few pages help you to ask yourself what you want from life. What kind of work and lifestyle suit you, for example, or what type of job and relationships would support the direction you want to take. Once you have answered these important questions, other things will start falling into place. You will be better able to set priorities, and balance the many aspects of your life. You'll also reduce unnecessary conflict and uncertainty over how to use your time. Your "Big Picture" will help you discover what you really want to do and will help motivate you to do it.

Defining your dreams as goals gives them form and structure

Define Your Goals

For some people, the process of defining goals can be an eye-opener, forcing them to focus for the first time on what they really want in life. But for most people, it is more of a process of clarification. Goals help you to see forward progress, in what might previously have seemed a long, pointless grind – and this gives you confidence to strive towards higher, more difficult goals.

We all have dreams. And whether we are aware of it or not, most of us have been thinking about our Life Goals all our lives but, for various reasons, we are often unwilling to write them down. However, there are some very good reasons for doing so.

TIP **Set sharp, clearly defined goals so that you can measure and take pride in their achievement.**

The Goal-Setting Process

The primary tool required to define your Big Picture is the setting of long-term "Life Goals". The simple, four-step procedure detailed below will help you to collect, clarify, and refine these goals.

This process of goal setting is a standard technique used by top-level athletes, successful business-people, and achievers in all fields – and a written **Life Goals Statement** is the cornerstone of any successful time-management programme. When dreams are acknowledged as "goals" in this way, they start to take on a definite and structured form. They no longer remain mere dreams; rather, they become aspirations that give a clear meaning, motivation, and direction to your life. They provide the measuring stick against which to gauge other activities as they come along.

→ Without a process like goal setting, it is far too easy to delay the actions that turn your dreams into reality. A written statement of goals brings you up against the fact that your time – and indeed your life – is a limited commodity.

→ The realization of the limits on your time, though a little scary, should jolt you into becoming more productive.

→ By going through this four-step goal-setting process, you will identify your most important wants, and cut away the distractions that slow you down and destroy your focus.

Break Down the Process

Create your Plan 60

⬇

Create your Five-Year Plan

⬇

Do a Reality Check

⬇

Write your Top Life Goals

Get It Down on Paper

Writing down your Life Goals forces you to make them concrete and specific. When the goals remain in your head, it is easy to get caught in the trap of delaying the activities you promised yourself you'd undertake. A written **Life Goals Statement** highlights the fact that your time – indeed, your life – is limited, and that you need to take prompt action if you are going to realize your goals.

Recognize the Opportunities

Some people feel that writing down a goals statement robs life of spontaneity and limits their options, but defining goals does not necessarily mean closing yourself off from opportunities. On the contrary, it helps you to recognize the right opportunities when they arise and save you from wasting precious time on low-value, low-priority tasks. More than this, as you start your journey towards achieving worthwhile and significant goals, you will start building up new skills and experience. The longer you go on, the more self-confidence you will gain. As a self-confident, successful, recognized expert, you will find that a whole range of great new opportunities open themselves

think
SMART

The next time that you are waiting for inspiration to strike, remember: a little effort and focus can do more to stimulate creativity than any amount of daydreaming.

That sudden flash of inspiration may feel spontaneous – but reflect on when you've achieved something truly remarkable or worthwhile in the past. Most likely, these things were achieved with forethought, planning, and long-term, determined effort. So, by all means keep time for spontaneity in your life. But make sure that you also make plenty of time for sustained, properly thought-through, goal-focused activity.

CASE study: Focusing on Priorities

Financial pressures had forced Rita to leave college at 21 and start work, but she promised herself she would return to college later to continue her studies. A decade passed, and she had still not taken action on her long-standing "Go Back to College" dream.

Now a 32-year-old marketing executive, Rita recently attended a Time Management seminar and was asked to write down her Life Goals statement. Starting a family and attending college both featured high on her list. This made Rita realize that if she wanted both goals to materialize, she'd have to take action on at least one of them in the near future. She did not want the stress of coping with babies in college, so she decided to give priority to taking a degree course. And that is what she is now doing.

• *Although Rita had long known that completing her education was important to her, she had allowed short-term urgencies to interfere with long-term goals. Her goals remained vague and therefore unrealized aspirations.*
• *Writing down her Life Goals statement forced Rita to focus on her priorities and set a sensible time-frame for their realization. This process of clarification made her realize that she needed to take immediate action in order to avoid missing out on the opportunity altogether.*

to you. What's more, as a genuine expert, you will deserve success when you take advantage of these opportunities.

Setting Life Goals will help you to bring your future into your present by giving you a clearer view of what your ideal future looks like. It will help you to retain perspective, focus your efforts, prioritize, motivate, and encourage you to achieve. And remember that the option to revise your goals is always open to you. After all, this is not a static exercise – an intrinsic part of goal setting is periodically reviewing your goals.

> **Don't judge each day by the harvest you reap, but by the seeds that you plant.**
>
> Robert Louis Stevenson

Formulate Your Plan 60

Your Plan 60 is a statement of where you want to be when you turn 60. It is the first stage in a four-step procedure that leads to your Life Goals Statement.

Look to the Future

Begin by visualizing your life at the age of 60. If you have already turned 60, or if this point does not seem far enough in the future, pick another more suitable birthday. Starting with the categories listed on the next page, consider all the important areas of your life and imagine that you can be, do, and have anything you want. What does your life look like? Forget about the logistics at this point. Take 30 minutes to brainstorm your dreams, however unrealistic, and write them out as a list. Then, whittle these down to your most important dreams.

Turn "Wants" into Goals

Now you have a list of "wants", the next step is to turn them into goals – active, concrete statements of your "wants", expressed in a "to be..." or a "to have..." format. A useful way of making goals more powerful is to use the **SMART** mnemonic: ensure that each of your goals is **Specific, Measurable, Attainable, Relevant,** and **Time-bound**. For example, you might want to become a CEO. Express this as: "To be CEO of such-and-such an organization by 1 January, 2025." Once you have created this goal list, you will probably be able to feel how much more powerful your "wants" have become, now that they are fixed goals.

Define Your Plan 60 Goals

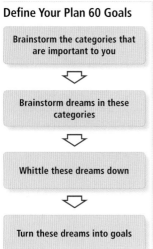

Brainstorm the categories that are important to you

⬇

Brainstorm dreams in these categories

⬇

Whittle these dreams down

⬇

Turn these dreams into goals

Focus Your Goals

If you try to achieve too many goals, you will most likely spread yourself so thinly that you achieve none. Cut away all but the most important goals.

One problem that people generally run in to during this exercise is that they have so many interests and desires they find it hard to define their goals. It's like being a kid in a chocolate factory. But it is important to zero in on one specific goal in each category. If you don't, you will start to lose focus.

→ Start by grouping your goals and dreams into categories that cover all of the critical areas in your life. These will probably include all of the general categories listed here, but if there are other areas of your life that strike you as important, include these headings too.

→ If you are finding it hard to make choices, try the "one-for-now" approach. Make a list of all the things you want to do in one category and then pick one goal to achieve "for now". This does not mean that you are eliminating the others: it simply indicates that, at this point in time, this particular goal is the one that is the most important to you. If you really want to include two tips in one category, that's fine too – so long as you keep your list short and focused.

Critical Categories

AREA OF LIFE

Self

Family

Romance

Friendships

Career

Finances

Health

Community

Spirituality

Others

TIP **Goal statements often seem more real if they are expressed in the present tense: "It is 31 December 2021, and I have a net worth of £5,000,000".**

Formulate Effective Goals with SMART

	Weak Goals	Powerful goals
Specific	To be happy	To have saved enough money for a comfortable retirement
Measurable	To be rich	To have a net worth of £1,000,000
Attainable	To discover a cure for cancer	To complete a sponsored marathon in aid of cancer charities
Relevant	For more people to recycle their rubbish	To be an active member of an environmental movement
Time-Bound	To achieve this goal before I am old	To achieve this time-bound goal by 31 December 2021

Share Your Aims

When considering goals, it is a good idea to enlist the help of your partner or friends. They know you well and may be able to help spot whether you are missing out on anything important. If you are part of a couple, it may make sense for both you and your partner to do this exercise together. This way you will be able to work out between you whether your goals are in alignment. If not, you can always change your list.

Deal with Conflicting Goals

Some of the goals on your list may conflict. If your goal is to become a CEO, for example, this is likely to get in the way of spending more time with your family. This conflict may, perhaps, still have the benefit of pushing you to increase the *quality* of the time you spend on each goal – but if you think it will cause frustration, it is best to spend some time trying to understand and resolve this conflict.

Goal conflicts can generally be resolved by setting priorities. Decide which goals are most important to you at this time. If you find it difficult to choose between two conflicting goals, ask yourself which of them you would choose if you could have only one. Finally, pick the five goals in your list that are most important to you right now. Don't feel guilty if you pick "becoming CEO" over spending

y Plan 60 goals are:

lf: *To have walked the Inca Trail and climbed Mt. Kilimanjaro*

mily: *To have a house in the country, two happy kids, and a dog*

mance: *To have a good marriage*

iendships: *To have a small group of close friends*

areer: *To be CEO of a successful international consulting firm*

inances: *To have paid off all my loans*

lealth: *To be in A-1 shape, with a weight less than 155 pounds*

Community: *To be an active member of an environmental movement*

Spirituality: *To practise half an hour of daily meditation*

more time with family. Just because becoming CEO is your goal now, does not mean that your family is unimportant to you. It simply means that, at this point in time, your focus is on becoming CEO. By next year, the focus may change.

Plan 60 Goals Consider every aspect of your life, and write down your "wants" in various categories. Once you have a list like the one above, you can narrow them down into your top five.

My Top Plan 60 Goals

When you have picked your five most important goals – ideally in just five separate categories – write them down in this grid. These are your top goals to achieve by the time you are 60. Once you have listed your top five goals, you may find that you have various goal conflicts to work through. If this is the case, you will need to set priorities to resolve the situation.

My goals

1 _____

2 _____

3 _____

4 _____

5 _____

Focus on the Medium Term

The next steps to working out your Life Goals involve getting a little more realistic. Instead of looking decades ahead, focus on the next few years.

Identify Your "Five-Year Plan" Goals

Where are you now, and where would you like to be in the next five years? Repeat the goal-setting exercise that you carried out for Plan 60. Again, the list can be as long as you wish, but this exercise requires you to think in practical terms. After all, there is only so much you can realistically achieve in the next five years.

Moving in the Same Direction?

The chances are that you will find your choices more or less in harmony with the priorities that you sketched out in your Plan 60. If they are not, get ready to undertake some major changes in your lifestyle: if the next five years are not moving you towards your Plan 60, it is time you did something about it!

When you have set your goals, pick the five that are most important to you and – just as you did with your Plan 60 – write them down as a separate list of Top "Five-Year Plan" Goals using the grid below.

My Medium-Term Goals

My Top "Five-Year Plan" Goals	My Top "Reality Check" Goals
1	1
2	2
3	3
4	4
5	5

CASE study: Conflicting Goals

When setting his Plan 60 goals, Peter Tsang identified a strong desire to help people make the most of their lives. However, when he started to think about his Five-Year Plan, he realized that he was at a stage of his life where he needed to build skills for his own long-term career success. As a result, his Five-Year Plan goals related exclusively to his career and contributed little to the way he wanted to live his life. Peter subtly changed his direction. He took his existing skill, but switched to an industry that more directly helped the people he wanted to help. And he started doing voluntary work, focused on his goals.

• Peter found that his first pass at a Five-Year Plan did not connect to his life goals. But by switching jobs, he could continue to build his career while also doing worthwhile work.
• By doing voluntary work focused on his lifetime goals, he started moving towards them. And because his career and voluntary work were now aligned, he found that one helped him in the other.

Take a Reality Check

This is "Step Three" of the Life Goals exercise, and it is a simple one: imagine that you have only one year to live. How would you like to spend this year? This exercise imposes a stringent reality check. It forces you to take an inventory of your life. Are there things that are important to you that you are not currently doing?

Choose Your Top "Reality Check" Goals

Again, use the approach we described previously to draw up a list of goals in the major life categories. This time, the list may not be as holistic as before. Write it down anyway and select the five immediate goals that are most important to you. If the new list consists of a completely different set of goals from the ones on your other lists, then the likelihood is that you need to make some real changes in your life. However, with proper time management, there is no reason why you should not start doing at least some of your preferred activities right away.

Identify Your Life Goals Statement

By now, you should have identified lots of important goals in many different categories. But since we are still prioritizing, it is time to make the final cut.

Whittle Them Down

The paradox about priorities is that if you have too many of them, they can't all be priorities. We have resolved this during the first three stages by using the "one for now" approach and selecting the five most important goals at the end of each exercise – but, we are still left with 15 goals. This is too many to focus on. You are now going to whittle them down to your five top Life Goals, which will become your Life Goals Statement.

Life Goal Scrapbook
Review and re-evaluate your Life Goals periodically. To help you do this, you could keep a scrapbook of cuttings and pictures that inspire you.

My Top Life Goals

When you have picked your five most important Life Goals from the goals on your other lists, write them down in this grid. You have now made your Life Goals Statement. This is the first and most important step towards regaining control of your time. These goals should form the foundation stone on which to build your time management programme.

My goals

1 _____

2 _____

3 _____

4 _____

5 _____

Select the five goals that seem most important to you. Feel free to choose any five goals from your list as your Life Goals – you have not permanently dropped the others, it is just that they are not now top priority. Make sure you bring your decision to a timely close, however, otherwise you risk procrastination and "paralysis by analysis".

Challenge Your Goals... And Commit

Spend a few minutes thinking carefully about these goals and refining the wording. Use the tips in this chapter to phrase them in as powerful and compelling a way as possible. Then, challenge any uncertainty rationally. When you are happy with your goals, write them down. Then, decide to commit yourself to achieving them.

The Life Goals Statement is not a static declaration and should be revised periodically. Add – or delete – items on your goals list at any time. Choose a set date annually to re-evaluate your Life Goals Statement and assess how the last year has brought you closer to achieving those goals.

> **Until one is fully committed, there is hesitancy, the chance to draw back... the moment one definitely commits oneself, then providence moves too.**
>
> Johann Wolfgang von Goethe

Summary: Setting Goals

The purpose of this chapter has been to help you identify the goals that should be shaping your life – because once you know where you are going and how you want to get there, you have priorities. These goals become a yardstick against which to evaluate the use of your time, and are therefore a key tool for managing your time.

Plan of Action

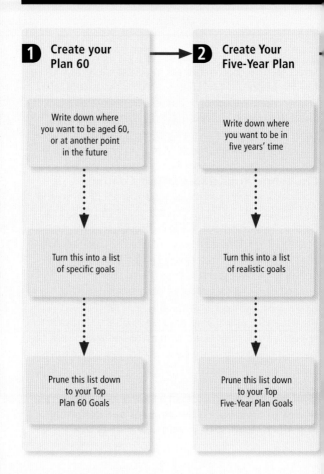

1 Create your Plan 60

Write down where you want to be aged 60, or at another point in the future

↓

Turn this into a list of specific goals

↓

Prune this list down to your Top Plan 60 Goals

2 Create Your Five-Year Plan

Write down where you want to be in five years' time

↓

Turn this into a list of realistic goals

↓

Prune this list down to your Top Five-Year Plan Goals

3 Take a Reality Check → **4** Create Your Life Goals Statement

Imagine you have just one year to live. What would you want to do?

↓

Turn this into a list of your most important goals

↓

Prune this list down to your Top Reality Check Goals

Look at your three lists of five goals – which are the most important?

↓

Prune these 15 goals down to your Top Five Life Goals

↓

Challenge your goals, and then commit to them

Organize 2
Your Life

This chapter helps you to evaluate the work you are engaged upon and explores the tools and strategies that you can use to convert your tasks into effective, productive activity. It will also help to ensure that the tasks that you do during your everyday life will contribute towards your bigger Life Goals. In this chapter, you will find out how to:

- Formulate an Action Programme to help you organize all of your projects
- Use brainstorming aids to help you ensure your Action Programme is comprehensive
- Review and schedule your work so that you can move towards your Life Goals
- Organize your physical and electronic workspace for maximum productivity.

Create Your Action Programme

You may already use To-Do lists to organize your work. These are a good start, but as you take on more complex projects, an Action Programme gives you a more effective way to evaluate, manage, and prioritize your daily tasks.

Choose the Right Tasks

Most of the activities we do on a daily level do not contribute towards our Life Goals. But to become fully effective, it is crucial that we forge a connection between life goals and daily tasks. Of course, none of us has total control over our work – we all have to cope with essential, often tedious activities. But how often do we stop and think about a job – whether we want to do it, how it fits in with our scheme of things – before we take it on? An **Action Programme** can help to evaluate and prioritize your daily tasks.

> A fully comprehensive To-Do list will help de-clutter your mind

Collect Together Actions

Begin by listing all the things in your world that need resolution. Try to collect and write down everything – urgent or not, big or small, personal or professional – that is incomplete and needs action from you to get done.

To some extent, this collection happens automatically. At work, e-mail requests are stored in your account, memos are delivered to your in-tray, mail reaches your mailbox, and messages accumulate on your voice mail. But there are also things percolating in your head, projects you want to run, things you intend to deal with, and ideas written

> **Being busy does not always mean real work. The object of all work is production or accomplishment... Seeming to do is doing nothing.**
>
> Thomas Edison

The Action Programme Process

As the chart on the right shows, creating the Action Programme is a four-step process. When you create your Action Programme for the first time, it may seem like a lengthy process. But once it is done, you should feel much more in control. It will also take little effort to update it on a routine basis. It may be easier to keep your Action Programme in a word processor file or a spreadsheet: this will make it quicker to input changes.

The Four-Step Process

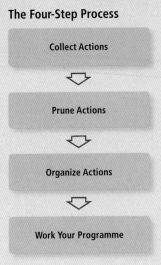

Collect Actions

Prune Actions

Organize Actions

Work Your Programme

down on stray bits of paper. All of this needs to be gathered up and put in place, too. By putting everything into your Action Programme, you can free your mind of nagging concerns and ensure that you prioritize actions coherently.

Prune Your List

Once you have created this comprehensive To-Do list, carefully consider each item and decide whether or not you need to take action.

- If you feel that you might need to take action on a particular item at some future date – or you might need to refer to the material later – store them in an assigned home for future reference.
- In instances where you do need to take action, identify the logical next action and write it down.
- If you'll never need to take action on it, delete it.

Pareto's Principle

This principle suggests that 80 per cent of the results we achieve are generated by just 20 per cent of our effort. To put it another way, 80 per cent of our effort goes into generating just 20 per cent of our results. To rise above this rule, you must not only focus your efforts on high-return tasks but also ensure you do not waste valuable time on low-priority, low pay-off tasks.

Organize the Actions

The Action Programme is split up into three parts:

1 **The Project Catalogue** is an inventory of all of the projects you are engaged in, and the small individual tasks that you have identified so far that contribute to them.

2 **The Next Action List** is the list of project tasks you want to work on today or this week. It shows the next actions you are going to take to move your projects forward.

3 **The Delegated Actions List** consists of projects and actions delegated to other people. Include details on who those people are and the date on which you will review progress.

1 The Project Catalogue

As you assess the actions on your list, you will probably find that some seem virtually to organize themselves into projects. A project is a list of tasks that intuitively belong together. For example, items like "Get new carpets", "paint study windows", and "fix shed door" can be grouped together into a "Do up the house" project. Move them into the Project Catalogue as a group. Organize the items that are part of the project as bullet points beneath the project name.

2 Next Actions

Look at these projects and identify which ones you are going to work on first. Next, for each of these, pinpoint the activity that you need to perform to start work on the project. If it can be done quickly, transfer it to the Next Action List. If not, break it down into a series of brief tasks, and transfer the first task to the Next Action List. For example, if your Next Action is to write an article, break this down into research, planning, writing, and editing phases. Make the research phase your Next Action, and put the rest in your Project Catalogue.

Keep your next actions small and achievable. This helps to keep up momentum and enhances your sense of having had a productive day. Don't put too many actions on your list. If you do, prioritize them from A to F, ranking them by importance, value, urgency, and relevance to your Life Goals, and remove the least important actions.

Group Actions into Projects

Actions to be grouped

⬇   ⬇

Project 1: Renovate the Attic   **Project 2: Sort Out the Garden**

The Project Catalogue It can be difficult to keep track of all the tasks and to-dos floating around in our heads. Many of these, however, naturally group into larger projects, making the individual actions much easier to keep track of and prioritize.

3 Delegated Actions

If you can delegate the action, then make the action of delegation your next action. Once you have delegated the action, it goes on your Delegated Actions List, together with a note of the person to whom you have delegated it and the date of your agreed checkpoint for the action.

Review Your Next Actions

Now check your Next Action List. If it is too cluttered, move some of the less urgent jobs back into the Project Catalogue. If it is thin or under-challenging, pull up some Next Actions from the Project Catalogue.

Revise and update the Next Action List regularly

Periodically monitor your success in dealing with these actions. If you find that any actions are stagnating on your list, consider whether you should cancel these projects, put them on hold, or raise their priority so that you deal with them.

Work Your Action Programme

Typically an **Action Programme** can run to many pages, but you don't have to run through the entire programme every day. You will usually be dealing with just the top pages, showing Next Actions and Delegated Actions. Some activities may be day-specific or time-specific. They can be either maintained as the top page of your Action Programme or marked on your calendar.

Make sure that the **Action Programme** works by reviewing the list periodically, deleting or archiving items you have completed, moving items from the Project Catalogue to the front pages as projects advance, and adding any new material that comes in.

TIP If the Next Action is going to take less than a couple of minutes, do it right away.

Arrange Your Action Programme

Although your Action Program will contain many actions and may run to several pages, this very simplified example should give you a feel for the way that your list will be arranged into Next Actions, Delegated Actions, and Projects.

This approach helps you to maintain focus on daily jobs and long-term goals simultaneously. It also ensures you always have a "next action" plan that you can implement or renegotiate, as well as a list of medium and long-term projects. The top pages ("Next Actions") are similar to a To-Do List. The other pages (particularly the "Project Catalogue") track the longer-term projects.

PROJECT CATALOGUE
Action Programme: updated 12/08

Article on Health Care Packages
(Project 10033)
- Source photographer
- List local hospitals
- Get telephone numbers
- Arrange interviews

DELEGATED ACTIONS
Action Programme: updated 12/08

- Monitor sourcing of photographer –
  Delegated to David – by 10 a.m. Tuesday

NEXT ACTIONS
Action Programme: updated 12/08

- List local hospitals

Capture Hidden Actions

For it to be effective in helping you to plan your time, your Action Programme has to be comprehensive. Unfortunately, it is all too easy to forget about whole areas of activity. This is why we use Trigger Lists.

Create Your Trigger Lists

You probably found the process of taking an inventory of your actions a painstaking, time-consuming exercise – and surprisingly tricky. Even though you jot down all the projects and tasks that seem to be running through your head, once you begin processing them, another one comes to mind. And when you think you have finally written everything down, there is the nagging worry that you have missed one out. "Trigger lists" help you to unearth them all.

These are various lists of categories that provide a "trigger" to find hidden actions that you may have left out. Use them to jog your memory about the type of activities that you must do on a regular basis, so that you can ensure that they are in your Action Programme.

TECHNIQUES *to* practise

A good technique to help you identify all of your professional triggers is to note down each step of your working process in turn.

- Depending on your job, this could start with the first time you talk to a client about doing some work, and end when you have confirmed that the final payment has cleared in your bank account. Each step in this process is a trigger.

- Then think about the work you have to do to support this process: ordering supplies, recruitment, administration, maintenance, and so on. These are also triggers.

- Alternatively, try running through your day from first thing in the morning until the moment you leave the office. Any jobs and actions that recur on a regular basis might act as useful triggers.

Possible Triggers

Imagine you are an interior designer with an active social life. You could split your triggers into two main category lists: personal and professional. The idea of these lists is simply to provide a trigger to unearth actions that are buried in your mind. Now update your Action Programme with the hidden actions you have flushed out.

PERSONAL	PROFESSIONAL
Friends	Clients
Birthdays	Drafts
Anniversaries	Paints
Plans	Design schemes
House	Finances
School	Computer
Errands	Phone calls
Finances	Ongoing projects
Clothes	Pending projects

Brainstorm the Categories

To put together your Trigger lists, brainstorm the types of activities you do on a regular basis and then list them in categories. Some categories are fairly common, in the sense that they are the type of activities that most people need to do in their day-to-day lives. For example:

• Phone calls you must make
• Co-workers you must talk to
• Reports to write
• Presentations you must make
• Meetings to attend or run.

Others categories may be more job-specific. If, for example, you are an event manager, these could be:

• Venues to book
• Upcoming events to prepare for
• Performers to book
• Invitations to issue.

Update Your Action Programme

Once you have listed all the categories that best match your circumstances, use the lists to seek out any actions that you may have missed when you were putting together your **Action Programme**. Then update the Action Programme using the hidden actions that you have flushed out.

Introduce Your A-Activities

It is time to re-introduce the key element that has so far been missing from the Action Programme – your Life Goals. Your A-Activity List sets out those activities that will take you towards your life goals.

Input Your Priorities

Having identified the Life Goals on which your time management is to be founded, now is the time to feed these into your **Action Programme**. The A-Activity List will help you to build a list of activities that will move you towards your Life Goals (we call these "A" activities as they are some of the most important activities you'll undertake). You can then build these into the **Action Programme**.

Prepare Your Life Goal Worksheet

Write one of your Life Goals at the top of a sheet of paper and then list the actions that you will need to take to achieve that particular goal. First, list the major actions. Then, break the major action that logically comes first into smaller actions. Keep breaking this action down until you have a series of small actions that will take no more than two hours each to complete. Do this for each of the other four goals on your **Life Goals Statement**.

think SMART

Visualize the steps you need to take in order to achieve your goals. Walking through them in your mind will make them seem more concrete.

Start keeping a file of things that help you visualize your goals. From now onwards, cut pictures out of magazines, collect brochures, visit exhibitions, and so on. Have fun building up a really strong image of that fantastic house in the countryside, or of the boat that's going to carry you around the world. And let yourself daydream (occasionally!)

Be Realistic

The chances are that when you have completed this process you will have a huge list of activities and not nearly enough time for them all. You need to set priorities. Switch from imaginative to realistic mode, and use these criteria to prioritize your activity list:

- Which of these activities is likely to yield the highest returns?
- Which of these will move you closest to your main Life Goals?
- Which of these activities are the most do-able in the near future?

Add in Your Life Goals

Once you have pruned all five Life Goal activity lists,

5 minute FIX

If you didn't have the time to formulate your goal lists before creating the Action Programme – perhaps you skipped straight to this chapter – take five minutes to brainstorm your Life Goals.

- Note down everything you'd like to achieve before you die.

- Note down a list of what you'd like to achieve over the next five years.

- Cross off or rethink anything that seems totally unrealistic.

- From this list choose your top-five goals – the goals that seem most important to you now – and use these to produce your A-Activities.

you will have your list of "A" Activities. Add the Life Goals as projects to the Project Catalogue section of your **Action Programme** (put them at the top of the project list, so that you keep their significance clearly in front of you.) Underneath, list the A-Activities that belong to each life goal. Finally, move the first action from each Life Goal Project onto your Next Action List. Now you are starting to achieve your aim – working towards your Life Goals has become an everyday part of your life!

TIP **Conduct an annual review for each Life Goal as one of the Project Catalogue actions. This helps to make goal-setting an ongoing part of your life.**

Categorize Your Work

At any given point in time, you can be engaged in three categories of work – organization, doing predefined work, and reacting to unplanned work. Evaluate your work in terms of these three categories and then judge whether the balance between them is right or wrong. If you are spending too little time on the second category and too much on the third, you will need to take corrective action.

Organizational Work, such as preparing your Action Programme or schedule, is essential to help you plan your time, including time to work towards your Life Goals.

Predefined Work, such as the work on your Action Programme, should take you towards your Life Goals. Make sure you spend enough time on this type of work.

Unplanned Work needs attention, but doesn't necessarily take you nearer your goals. It can be unavoidable, so try to build it into your schedule where possible.

Evaluate Your Workload

This tool helps you to understand your daily work pattern and makes it easier to change it so that you become more effective.

Is Your Plan is Working?

Your **Action Programme** is in place, and you are using it to plan your time. However, you also need to exert the correct level of control over your work. Evaluating your work means making sure that you have a good balance between routine tasks and high-value actions that move you towards your Life Goals. There are two elements to this.

- The first step involves categorizing your work to make sure that you have the right balance between predefined work, organization, and responding to work as it shows up.
- The second approach involves thinking about whether your daily actions genuinely carry you towards your goals. Take the time to review your daily activities: how many of them are in alignment with your Life Goals? If the answer is "Not very many", then this is an important wake-up call. Perhaps it is time that you built more goal-related activities into your schedule.

CASE study: Evaluating Goals

Rahul set himself a goal of losing weight by running three times a week at lunchtime. The goal was in his Action Programme, and the run was clearly marked in his schedule. However, he found it difficult to get out of the office: meetings over-ran, people dropped in to chat, and work needed to be finished.

Rahul rethought his priorities. He made an effort to schedule meetings so that they started earlier, gave plenty of notice of when he would be running, and pushed himself to get out of the office. Within ten weeks he hit his ideal weight.

- *Rahul was letting routine tasks override an Life Goal. But, because he kept his goals in clear view, he could see he wasn't achieving them and retake control.*
- *Because he had managed other people's expectations well in advance, they adjusted quickly and easily to his new routine.*

Create Your Schedule

Scheduling is the process by which you look at the time available to you, and plan how you will use it to achieve the goals you have identified.

Make Use of the Time Available

So far, we have focused on priorities and goals. These define what you aspire to do with your time. Scheduling is where these aspirations meet the hard reality of the time you have available. It's the tool you must use to make time for your priorities and to cut out things that are low priority. Scheduling is best done on a regular basis, such as at the start of each week. By using a schedule properly, you can:

- Understand what you can realistically achieve with your time, and plan to make the best use of your time
- Preserve contingency time to handle "the unexpected"
- Minimize stress by avoiding over-commitment
- Ensure that there's room to keep on achieving your Life Goals.

Choose the Right Tools

Start by choosing a scheduling format that suits your preferences. Diaries, calendars, paper-based organizers, PDAs, and integrated software suites such as MS Outlook are all useful scheduling tools. Choose the one that best suits your situation, current job structure, taste, and budget. The key qualities are that you should be able to enter data easily and view an appropriate span of time at the correct level of detail.

Prepare Your Schedule

Preparing a robust schedule is easy, provided that you are methodical in your approach – the key point is to be rigorous in eliminating work you do not have time to do.

Firstly, identify the time you want to make available for your work. This will depend on the way your job is structured and on your personal life goals. Then identify the actions that you absolutely must complete in order to do a good job. These will often be the key things against which you are assessed.

→ Allow time to communicate with your boss and key people. Your best time management efforts will be derailed if you do not set aside time for the important people in your life.

→ Leave ten minutes every day in your schedule to organize yourself, maintain your time management systems, and keep focused on the real priorities in your life.

→ Block in appropriate contingency time. Usually, the more unpredictable your job, the more contingency time you need.

→ Review your Next Actions List, and schedule in the high-priority urgent activities, as well as the essential maintenance tasks.

After scheduling, you are left with "discretionary time" – this is the time available to deliver your priorities and achieve your goals. Review your Next Action lists and A-Activity lists, evaluate the time needed to achieve these actions, and schedule them in.

Effective Scheduling Techniques

HIGH IMPACT
- Being realistic with completion dates and levels of importance
- Completing tasks by their priority
- Not being put off by difficult or unappealing tasks

NEGATIVE IMPACT
- Giving priority to tasks simply because you enjoy them
- Leaving important elements out
- Setting unrealistic time-frames that always need to be amended

Review Your Work

Here comes the catch. By the time you have finished your schedule, you will probably find that you simply don't have any discretionary time at your disposal. If this is the case, you need to conduct a thorough review of your work. You must be ruthless if you want to make the schedule work.

After all, your Life Goals are under threat: if anything is standing in the way of achieving these goals, they must be dealt with, at once.

To do this, turn your attention to your **Action Programme** and schedule. Purge actions wherever you can (without sacrificing Life Goals). For example, ask yourself: Does that job really need to be done? Is there anything I can delegate? What can I hire out? Examine all of your options. If necessary, consider lowering your standards for certain To-Dos.

Break Down Your Schedule

Identify the time you have available for your work

⬇

Schedule in time to communicate with colleagues and other key people

⬇

Schedule in at least 10 minutes each day for organization and maintenance

⬇

Schedule in high-priority, urgent tasks from your Next Actions list

⬇

Block in appropriate contingency time

⬇

Review your schedule: look for ways to delegate, automate, or outsource tasks

Have Alternative Strategies

Remember, one of the most important ways you can learn to achieve success is by maximizing the "leverage" you can achieve with your time. Increase the amount of work you can do by delegating work to others, spending money on outsourcing time-consuming tasks, or using technology to

Renegotiate Your Workload

If, when you have pruned every aspect of your Action Plan, you still can't find time for your A-Activities, you may need to renegotiate your workload.

→ When renegotiating your workload, always factor in a little extra time beyond your contractual hours to "show willing".

→ Keep a log of what you spend your time on for two weeks, so you can use it as a reference when you estimate the communication and contingency time you need.

→ Ensure that task time estimates are reasonable, perhaps by basing them on how long similar jobs took previously.

→ Where seemingly simple jobs take a long time, break them down into smaller steps.

→ Before the meeting, list your roles and responsibilities – as you understand them – and identify those that you want to drop.

→ Plan how these could be handled. Perhaps you could outsource them or delegate them to an assistant.

automate as much of your work as possible – it will free you up to achieve your goals. For more information about delegating tasks and other ways to increase your leverage, turn to chapters four and five.

Are You Asking Too Much?

As well as reviewing the **Action Plan**, you should also go back to your A-Activity list and **Life Goals Statement**. Scrutinize them carefully. Have you set goals that just aren't achievable within the time you have available? Perhaps you are taking on too many additional duties?

There cannot be a crisis next week. My schedule is full.
Henry Kissinger

Summary: The Action Programme

The Action Programme is an effective way to tidy up and prioritize tasks and chores by organizing them into projects, picking out those actions that can be delegated, and identifying the next actions required to move each project along. It also provides a good way to incorporate your Life Goals into your daily activities.

Plan of Action

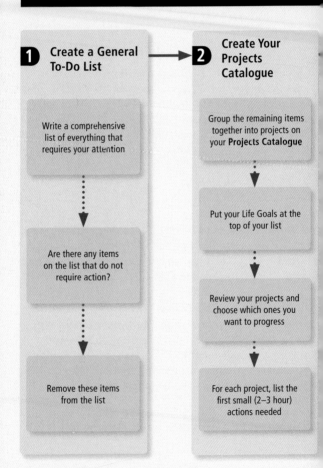

1 Create a General To-Do List

Write a comprehensive list of everything that requires your attention

Are there any items on the list that do not require action?

Remove these items from the list

2 Create Your Projects Catalogue

Group the remaining items together into projects on your **Projects Catalogue**

Put your Life Goals at the top of your list

Review your projects and choose which ones you want to progress

For each project, list the first small (2–3 hour) actions needed

3 Create Your Delegated Actions List → **4** Create Your Next Actions List

3 Create Your Delegated Actions List	**4** Create Your Next Actions List
Can any of these actions or projects be delegated?	Put all remaining undelegated actions on to your **Next Actions List**
Put these items onto your **Delegated Actions List**	Prioritize actions – move low priority actions back to the Project Catalogue
Arrange to delegate them. Next to each item add a review date and the name of the person delegated to	Update your Action Programme regularly

Use the Next Action Organizer

Now that the Action Programme is in place, you need an organization system that helps you to deal effectively with all of the stuff that enters your life and requires your attention each day.

Clear the Clutter

Even if you have all your goals and action plans mapped out, you will have trouble realizing them if you can't move past clutter. Clutter is anything that distracts you and takes up your time, energy, and space without yielding tangible results in return. It is stuff that you should have taken action on yesterday, but somehow didn't. And with every passing day, it is accumulating into a mess that is becoming increasingly difficult to tackle.

Clutter is physical mess – mail, memos, reports, newspapers, magazines, bills, proposals, plans, and promotional items, to name but a few of possible items – but it can be mental, too. All those disjointed thoughts that keep running through your head are mental clutter. They have no relevance to the job at hand; they are just stray thoughts – sometimes reminders, sometimes ideas – that randomly pop up in your mind.

The Price of Disorganization

Being unable to find the information you need is not only frustrating – it is inefficient and time-consuming. To get a monetary perspective on the situation, consider a report in the *Wall Street Journal* from March 1997, which found that the average US executive wastes one hour per day searching messy desks and files for misplaced information. This equates to six weeks a year or, at an annual salary of $60,000, nearly $8,000 per year of wasted organization money – per executive!

Desktop Clutter

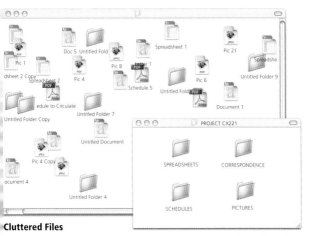

Cluttered Files

Organized Files

Organize your Desktop Clutter can be electronic, as well as mental or physical. Group related documents together on your desktop and organize your data into clearly labelled folders and sub-folders so that information can be found easily.

Avoid Distractions

Until you have made a note about something that you have to do (ideally adding it to your **Action Programme**) you tend to carry it in your head. But, there is only so much information that any one of us can retain at any one time – our "attentional capacity". If your attention is devoted to remembering diverse mental notes, it cannot be focused on the task at hand. Worse still, mental clutter tends to pop up to distract you at inappropriate times. Perhaps you are brainstorming on the new product launch but your mind keeps sending out little blips about that client you need to call. You can't possibly call him just now, but your mind has picked this as the best time to remind you. Irritating, isn't it?

TIP **Don't forget to schedule in time for admin and organization when you plan your work.**

Categories of Input

Within the Next Action Organizer, there are seven categories into which the inputs entering your life can be organized; these can be further divided into actionable and inactionable.

The three actionable categories – the Project Catalogue, the Next Action List, and the Delegated Actions List – form part of the Action Programme, which we have already covered. These categories look at inputs that require direct action from you or from people to whom you have delegated work. Four further categories cover inputs that are not directly actionable. These inactionable inputs are:

→ **Project Support Material** This comprises all the material – plans, proposals, and general information – that support your projects.
→ **Reference Material** This material is not actionable, but it is information that you might need someday. The trick here is to find a balance discarding useful material and storing junk.
→ **Someday/Maybe** This category comprises material you feel you might want to take action on someday. These are not essential items, but they are things you would like to add to your Action Programme at some future date.
→ **Trash** This is self-explanatory. All the inputs that come your way but have no personal relevance fall under this heading – promotional mailers, unread newsletters, and so on.

Action and Inactionable Inputs

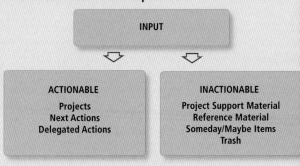

ACTIONABLE
Projects
Next Actions
Delegated Actions

INACTIONABLE
Project Support Material
Reference Material
Someday/Maybe Items
Trash

TIP **If you write down all your mental notes, you will improve your focus and effectiveness.**

Organize for Maximum Productivity

You need a comprehensive, effective organization system that helps you to collect, process, and track everything that comes in. The **Next Action Organization System** will do this for you. Although it takes time to set up, it will yield phenomenal returns. Its objective is to:

- Capture everything that needs to be done – now, later, someday – into a logical system.
- Process it and decide on action.
- Assign a place for, and keep track of it.

As well as eliminating clutter, you will be able to access the information quickly – as and when required. You will no longer waste time looking for missing papers, arriving at meetings without vital information, or being "ambushed" by urgent material lying forgotten, under a pile of papers.

Processing inputs as they arrive frees up time to focus on other tasks

Regain Your Time

Once you master the skills and habit of the **Next Action Organization System**, you will find yourself regaining control of both your time and your mind space. Time will be released because you will know just where everything is and when actions need to be taken. And mind space is freed up because there is a system in place to collect, process, and track things. When you can finally push distractions out of your mind and allot physical homes to the clutter that you carry in your head, your mind lets go of the lower-level job of hanging on to information, leaving you to concentrate your efforts on other, higher-value tasks – including the all-important pursuit of the A-Activities that take you towards your main life goals.

Process the Inputs

Now that you have the categories, the Next Action Organization System gives you a quick, effective process that you can use to decide how to process all inputs.

Take Total Control

The Input Processor enables you to manage, in a consistent and efficient way, anything new that comes to your attention – letters, e-mails, useful information, requests from your boss or from your clients, ideas for new products, and so on. Where you need to take action, it helps you to take the action, delegate it, or schedule it with certainty of follow-up. If you want to store information, the input processor helps you put it in the right place, for quick future recall. This tool helps you to stay on top of your paperwork; to remain totally in control, however complex your job; and to be reliable in meeting your commitments.

Whenever you receive an input, ask the following questions and process the input appropriately.

- Is the input part of a project, or does it initiate a project?
- Is the input actionable?

Process Projects

Here we define projects as tasks that need a number of actions to be carried out before the task is complete. If you have relatively few, simple projects, then you may be able to cope using just the Project Catalogue section of your **Action Programme**. With a larger number of projects, with more complex projects, or with projects

5 minute FIX

If you don't have time to organize computer files into properly structured directories, there is a useful shortcut.

The Google desktop search function on your computer will index all your files and e-mails. It also gives you a handy search box on your deskbar, so you can retrieve information quickly. This free tool can be installed by going to www.desktop.google.com.

Paperwork or PC?

It is obviously a duplication of effort to manage both a physical filing system and a computer-based filing system – in an ideal world, you would use one or the other exclusively. Unfortunately it takes time to scan physical information, just as it does to print out and file digital information. The best way forward depends on preference and on how you receive the majority of your inputs:

→ If you receive most of your inputs on paper, it probably make sense to maintain paper files and print off and file digital information when it arrives.
→ If you receive most of your inputs digitally, then scan in paper documents and store them digitally.
→ If, like many of us, you work with a mixture of on- and off-line material, then you may find it more effective to keep parallel paper and digital systems.

Remember that technology is only useful in so far as it makes life easier, so use whatever type of system feels most natural to you.

that require you to store paperwork, it is worth setting up an effective system of Project Support Files. This system should be updated with every project-related input that arrives.

TIP Ensure that large or complex projects get the attention and resources they require – particularly if they are time-critical.

As a project-related input arrives, first check to see whether the project exists in your Project Catalogue. If it relates to an existing project, update the Project Catalogue and Project Files appropriately. If the input relates to a new project, open up a new, consecutively numbered file for the project, and make a new entry for it (with the project number) on your Project Catalogue.

Process Actionable Inputs

Actionable inputs are processed by the **Action Programme** that we discussed earlier – take immediate action, defer it, or delegate the task and put it on your Delegated Actions List. Where you have decided to defer an action, update your **Action Programme** or your calendar appropriately.

Process Non-Actionable Inputs

Inputs that are not actionable fall into three categories:

- Trash should be thrown away, or shredded if confidential.
- Someday/Maybe inputs go into your Bring Forward File, filed for the month or day on which you want to review the input, or on the bottom of the list of projects in your Project Catalogue.
- Reference information needs to be stored appropriately in your Reference Files.

By following this approach, you should always know exactly where information is and you should always be well-organized and efficient, whatever the volume of work coming in to you.

TECHNIQUES *to* practise

You will think more clearly if you can clear your mind of distracting thoughts.

If you find yourself frequently distracted, carry a small notebook with you at all times. Whenever a distracting thought (a mental to-do, a worry, or an idea) pops into your mind, write it down and then, unless it's urgent, forget about it. Review this notebook each time you update your Action Programme:

- Add any to-dos in the right place in your Action Programme.
- Place your ideas as projects or sub-projects within it.
- For worries, schedule a time to evaluate them carefully – if they are valid, set up an Action Programme project to manage the risk. If not, analyze them rationally, and let them go. (If you are a worrier, you may find this "rescheduling worry" technique hugely liberating!)

As you work through the input processor, you will need to set up the physical system that supports it in order to manage your paperwork effectively.

Bring Forward File This is a 3-D version of a calendar used to manage those someday/maybe items. Label 12 files with the names of the months. If, in May, an item that doesn't need action until July crosses your desk, put it in the July file. When you pick up the file on 1 July you will be reminded about the action you need to take.

Reference Files How you organize these files depends on your job. For example, if you work in human resources, you may want reference files for individual staff members, but in accounts, you may want files for each customer. A backup, alphabetical filing system for material that does not fit with your main files can also be useful.

Project Files When you need to store papers relating to projects, it is worth setting up project files. Number your projects sequentially, and arrange the corresponding files in numerical order. By noting this number by the project details in your Project Catalogue, you will instantly know where to find information on that project.

Calendar This is used for recording day-specific and time-specific actions – it could be the calendar hanging in your cubicle, the one in your PDA, or even the one on your mobile phone. You could also sub-group the calendar actions in two categories – personal and professional – and keep them on separate calendars.

Summary: Processing the Inputs

Inputs are anything that comes to your attention – internal or external mail, e-mail, information, a request from your boss, ideas for new projects. Follow the steps in this SuperSummary to make sure that each and every input is dealt with appropriately, whether that means placing it in your action plan, taking immediate action, filing the information away for reference, or consigning the input to the trash.

Process the Inputs

Does the input require action? — YES

NO ↓

Process Non-Actionable Inputs

Will it need action at a specific point in the future? — YES ·····▶ Add to your **Bring Forward File** under the month or day you wish to review it

NO ↓

Do you need to keep it for future reference? — YES ·····▶ Add to your **Reference Files**

NO ↓

Can it be dumped? — YES ·····▶ Put in the trash

Process Actionable Inputs

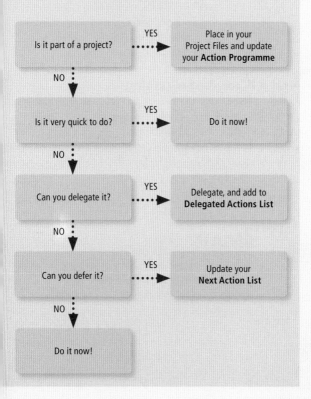

Is it part of a project? — **YES** ⟶ Place in your Project Files and update your **Action Programme**

NO

Is it very quick to do? — **YES** ⟶ Do it now!

NO

Can you delegate it? — **YES** ⟶ Delegate, and add to **Delegated Actions List**

NO

Can you defer it? — **YES** ⟶ Update your **Next Action List**

NO

Do it now!

Organize Your Work Space

The arrangement of your work space has a major impact on your effectiveness and productivity, but it is often overlooked as an aspect of time management.

Enjoy Easy Access To Resources

Try to locate your work space next to, or close to, the people and resources you need to work with so that you have easy access to them. Not only is this more efficient, but you will often find that you work more productively with these people as a result.

Make sure your reference files, project-support files, and bring-forward files are easily at hand. Ideally, you should be able to file or retrieve information without leaving your desk. This helps you to work faster and makes it easy to keep your systems up-to-date. It also ensures that any unnecessary paperwork is kept off your desktop.

Find A Place for Everything

Make sure you have the necessary files, partitions, in-trays, and other organizing devices to stay organized. Small expenditures can help you to be disproportionately more productive. If you need more work space, extend your desk or purchase a credenza and hutch. This will give you plenty of extra work surface and additional storage.

think
SMART

Once your accumulated mess is clear, try to set aside at least some time every day to keep your organization system clean, clear, and complete.

This is your Organizing Time. Usually about 15 minutes every day is sufficient for organizing yourself. Consciously block out this time on your schedule, write it in your diary as you would any other work commitment, and respect it in the same way.

Keep Your Desk Well-Ordered

Whether you are juggling with several different projects at once and need to access paper-based information quickly, or you are dealing with sensitive or confidential material, a well-organized desk is essential. It doesn't need to be spotlessly tidy, but you do need to be able to find what you want, when you want it.

In-tray contains incoming and current paperwork; documents are filed away regularly.

Telephone and contact book within easy reach.

If frequently used, monitor, keyboard, and mouse correctly placed to minimize strain.

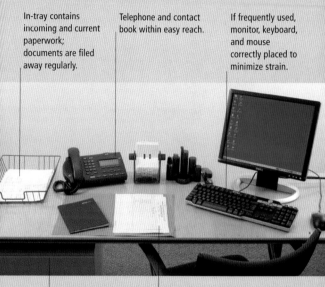

Properly organized filing system within easy reach.

Reference file open on desk. When work is complete, this will be dropped back into the reference file system.

A well-ordered desk is not necessarily clear. If you deal with many different things during a day, then it probably does make sense to file things away as you complete them, so you have space to work on the next thing. If you work on the same project for several days, however, it clearly wastes time if you put things away at the end of one day only in order to pull them out again at the start of the next. Adopt the approach that is most relevant to you.

CASE study: Organizing Information

Despite a high success rate with enquiries, Teiji, a helpdesk operator, received a low rating for organization in his appraisal. Reflecting on the reasons for this, he had to admit that he'd taken several minutes to find important documents the last few times his boss had asked for information. And he often floundered early on in a client call. Looking at the stacks of paper on his desk, he knew he had to do something. He implemented a filing system, reorganized the documents on his PC desktop, and used an indexing tool to index his e-mails. His next evaluation was much better.

• *Although his work was basically sound, Teiji was wasting the time of the people around him. This made him look sloppy, and disguised the quality of his work.*
• *By taking the time to organize information effectively, he was able to access it more quickly and get the answers people needed before they became impatient.*

Manage Your E-Mails

E-mail is the electronic equivalent of paper; if you don't set up an efficient system to deal with it, it will bury you. In the workplace, and sometimes even at home, e-mail can form a large part of the clutter that stands in the way of efficiency. For many people, the vast majority of inputs arrive by e-mail rather than on paper, and the input processor needs to be applied in just the same way.

Spam is the e-mail equivalent of junk mail. Set up your e-mail program to delete messages that come from known spammers. Many Internet Service Providers offer filtering services, but these can produce "false positives" that misclassify legitimate e-mails as spam. Sorting the mail in your inbox into message title order allows you to spot

> **Your mind, which is yourself, can be likened to a house. The first necessary move, then, is to rid that house of all but furnishings essential to success.**
>
> John MacDonald

spam quickly by subject, and once you've cleared out the spam you can reset the order. If you receive a lot of unwanted e-mails from non-spam sources, ask to be

TIP Do not become chained to e-mail – your computer should be your servant, not your master.

removed from their mailing lists. Review the newsletters you receive, and unsubscribe to those you no longer want. You could send out a message to all your acquaintances asking them not to send chain letters, jokes, and the like.

Sort the Real Mail

If you receive large amounts of e-mail, set up mailboxes within your e-mail program so that you can move incoming e-mails into appropriate mailboxes, depending on content. This allows you to prioritize your e-mail, and enables you to batch up particular types of e-mails so you can deal with them quickly and efficiently.

Don't Let It Rule You

If you succumb to the temptation of constantly checking your e-mail throughout the day, you will be continually distracted and you won't get much done. Instead, set a regular time to check and respond to e-mail. You can turn off the automatic notification facility or even close down your e-mail program completely.

Stay Protected

E-mail, for all its speed and convenience, has a major downside – the ability to transport viruses and other malevolent software into your computer. If you are part of a network, this risk can extend to the whole organization. Make it a priority to invest in good anti-virus software, such as Norton, McAfee, Sophos, or Symantec, and keep it updated. Remember – the cost of losing all your electronic data is too high a price to pay.

Overcome All The Obstacles

You have now identified your priorities, marked out plans and schedules to achieve them, and organized your life to support your mission. What could possibly hold you back? One answer is bad habits – either yours, or those of the people around you. In this chapter, we will see how to overcome some of the barriers that can steal your time, including:

- Interruptions, the demands on your time and attention that mean your agenda gets ignored
- Perfectionism, the loss of perspective that stops you recognizing when good is good enough
- Procrastination, the tendency to keep on putting off important tasks and activities.

Overcome the Barriers to Success

Once your plans are all in place, crunch time often comes when you try to put them into action. You may require concrete strategies to overcome these barriers.

Identify What is in the Way

Usually, the transition from planning to action happens smoothly. Yet there are times when you have a great plan but are just unable to move ahead on it. Your schedule tells you what to do, but you can't do it. What is holding you back?

> **Identify your own internal and external barriers to taking action**

If you have prioritized your activities successfully, all the support systems are in place to enable you to achieve your goals, and the clutter that stood in the way has been removed, the only barriers that can be standing in your way are other people or yourself. If you let these barriers to success sidetrack you from your plans, you will never get much accomplished. You need to identify the time-wasters and deal with them.

TECHNIQUES *to* practise

You may find it useful to make a regular review of what you've achieved each week – and what you haven't. Over the next few weeks, schedule in a 20-minute review for a quiet time each Friday. Use this period to reflect on what you planned to do during the week, and then look at what you actually achieved:

- Look at each action you failed to achieve, and write down what stopped you doing it.
- Question yourself about whether your reasons were valid.
- Try to identify any patterns – perhaps your goals were too ambitious, or you allowed too many interruptions.
- Draw conclusions and then take appropriate action.

The Three Barriers

Over the course of this chapter, we will analyze the major time bandits that block your efforts to keep to schedule. Most barriers can be classified under three main headings:

→ **Interruptions** Other people competing for your time and attention and throwing your schedule off course.
→ **Perfectionism** The lack of perspective that makes it difficult to recognize when a task is finished.
→ **Procrastination** Putting tasks off because they seem overwhelming, unpleasant, or because you feel unqualified.

Recognize the External Forces

Sometimes the obstacle is the outside world, which keeps intruding on the space you have reserved for your plan or your schedule. Let's suppose that you have just sat down at your desk to create a Trigger List when a colleague walks in. She wants your opinion on her project, so you set your list aside and start to help her. Half an hour flies by and you realize it is time for your meeting with a client. You rush off, and the Trigger List lies abandoned on your desk. Interruptions have won the day. Other people's needs and requests can stop you moving ahead with you own plans.

Understand Your Internal Impediments

Sometimes it is your own fears and worries, or aspects of your own character, that prevent you from proceeding with your plans or sticking to your schedule. Let's suppose you have identified romance as a priority area, and to accomplish this goal you plan to go for that "Singles Only" holiday. Yet when it comes to actually signing up for the holiday, you regretfully chicken out – the steps you need to take to reach your goal seem too overwhelming. It's no good simply telling yourself to stick to your schedule – you need to tackle the underlying causes of your procrastination.

Minimize Interruptions

Sometimes you can find that the people competing for your time and attention are so demanding, your own agenda gets buried under the flurry of interruptions.

Keep an Interrupters Log

Interruptions and crises are a part of everyone's normal day-to-day life. However, problems arise when these interruptions start to push you off schedule. If this happens a lot, try keeping a log of all visitors, phone calls, and other interrupters over the course of one week. Once you have the log results, analyze who these time-snatchers were and what they wanted.

Your interruptor's log will help you to decide whether or not an interruption is valid. If you feel a large proportion of them are valid, go ahead and schedule them. Earmark a slot in your daily plan to deal with these interruptions, which then become defined tasks, catered for in your schedule.

The Interruptor's Log

Person	Date / Time	Nature of interruption	Valid	Urgent
Tariq	Monday 09.55	Wanted to agree contents of Guzman proposal. 20 minutes.	✓	✓
Simon	Monday 10.40	Wants us to buy advertising. Pushy, not relevant. 10 minutes.	✗	✗
Janet	Monday 12:00	Advance planning for next quarter's product launch. 20 minutes.	✓	✗
Michael	Monday 12.20	Peter Springer query. Shouldn't have been escalated. 5 minutes.	✗	✓

Evaluate Interruptions The log is a useful tool to help you decide whether an interruption is valid; if most are, incorporate a regular slot into your schedule.

TIP When interrupted, take time to assess things clearly. Don't get rushed into decisions.

Understand the Manager's Role

Dealing with interruptions is part of a manager's job – some studies have shown that, on average, managers are interrupted every six minutes. If you are a manager, be careful how you cut down on interruptions. Your main job is to manage people, and dealing with interruptions is part of that job.

Make sure you are available for your team, and that you can act early enough to "nip problems in the bud". However, if you are also trying to deliver a significant amount of work at the same time, you may need either to delegate some of it or turn it away so that you have time to do your real job.

Recognize Real Emergencies

While some people do hype things up so that their pet projects get more attention than they deserve, some "interruptions" may be real emergencies that need immediate, focused activity. Similarly, interruptions may turn out to be opportunities that will advance you more quickly towards your goals if you grasp them. While you should stick to your schedule, don't be excessively rigid. Make sure that you deal with emergencies when they need attention, and take advantage of any opportunities that do arise.

Identify Which Interruptions Require Your Attention

> How valid is the interruption and how urgent is the task?

⬇

> How important to you – personally or professionally – is the person who is interrupting?

⬇

> How long will the interruption last and how much time do you have in your schedule?

⬇

> Can anyone else deal with the interruption instead of you?

Use Positive Delay

It is tempting to react instantly to interruptions, but a small delay in reacting to a request can help you to assess it accurately. In most

Deter Interruptions Arrange your workspace in a way that discourages people from interrupting your work. Point your chair away from the source of potential intrusions and use your arm and shoulder to form a barrier.

cases, you can safely postpone your response for a few minutes, if not longer. Use this breathing space to mentally run the request through the Input Processor, and then deal with the problem in action, rather than reaction mode.

Learn to Say "No"

It is impossible to do everything that everyone wants. There just isn't time. So you have to learn to say "no" – to at least some of the requests that come your way. Saying "no" isn't easy, but using this word promptly, properly, and politely can save you a great deal of time and frustration. It makes sense to prioritize interruptions. Consider both the person who is interrupting you and what is being asked of you. If both the person and the task are important, try to fit in the request. If only one of the two is important, check your schedule and see if you can make some time. Otherwise, say "no". Admittedly, it isn't easy. But the more you practise, the easier it will become. And remember that you don't have to be rude when saying "no" – refusing a request can be done gracefully and courteously.

If Necessary, Compromise

What do you do if the interrupter is someone important to you – your partner, your boss, your child, your parent, or your best friend – and you don't feel you can just say "no"? Look at the situation realistically and assess the request's importance to the other person. How much time will it take? Does it push you off schedule? Is this a pattern? Are you being reasonable? If you feel that the other person's request is a priority, but you still don't want to take it on, try to find a compromise. In this way, you can often satisfy people without completely sacrificing your own priorities.

Judge When to Say "No"

It is impossible to do everything that everyone wants. There just isn't time. You have to learn to say "no", at least to some of the requests that come your way, if you want to save your own day. When you are interrupted, run through the following checklist. Is the task the interrupter wants you to take on:

→ Unimportant?
→ One that can be done later?
→ One that can be done by someone else?
→ Something you simply don't want to do?

If so, it is one that you can often promptly and politely turn down.

Make Your Case

If there is a long-standing conflict between priorities, it is time to clarify your position. Remember that a major reason that people get promoted is that they have learned to deal with difficult situations in a calm, rational, and clear-headed way. While you may want to impress your boss by being flexible and hard-working, your boss should be sensible enough to know that there is only so much that you can take on before other work suffers. Also, if you are good at what you do, then he or she will not want to lose you to overwork and burnout.

Telephone Techniques

There is absolutely no need to stop whatever you are doing to answer the phone, every time it rings. A little technology and some basic discipline can go a long way towards helping you to escape the tyranny of the telephone.

- If you need time to concentrate, use an answering machine to screen your calls. If it is a genuine emergency, take the call. Otherwise, get back to the caller at your convenience.

- Schedule a specific time for making calls, preferably early in the day, and try to take the initiative in contacting the other person. This way, you can make the call according to your schedule, and interruptions will be automatically minimized.

- Practise the art of short phone calls. Get to the point quickly. Be clear and concise. Before dialling, decide what you intend to say. Listen attentively. Keep a pen and paper handy.

5 minute FIX

If you're in the middle of an important task and don't want to be disturbed, take a minute to make your workspace a little less welcoming to casual interruptions.

- Leave piles of papers, coats, or briefcases on chairs to make them seem unavailable to casual visitors.

- Rearrange furniture so that there's nowhere easy for people to settle when they come in.

Practise How to Say "No"

Turning down requests can, and should, be done in a positive and constructive way. Work out a set of stock responses to help negotiate your way through this situation.

Suppose that you have a workaholic boss who is constantly interrupting your work with new jobs, or pushing you beyond your limits. Each time you try to say "no" you find yourself sounding defensive, and worry that you don't seem committed to your job. Practise your stock responses at home in front of the mirror.

→ "Thanks for this opportunity. I want to do this job. Can it wait a little because I currently have X, Y, and Z on my plate?"

→ "I am so over-committed right now that I will not be able to do this job full justice."

→ "I want to handle this assignment, but I will have to drop X project to devote proper attention to it. What would you like me to focus on, X or this new assignment? Which can wait?"

→ "That sounds interesting – I'd like to do it. Can we look at my work schedule and decide which jobs are most important to you? I will work on them in that priority and we will get a realistic idea of what can be accomplished and by when."

Next time you feel your boss is being unreasonable, you will be able to make it clear, in a positive, constructive way, that while you take your job seriously, you already have a full workload.

Effective Ways to Say "No"

HIGH IMPACT

- Being calm and mature
- Being factual
- Having a well-thought-out schedule as evidence
- Being flexible; being prepared to renegotiate

NEGATIVE IMPACT

- Being aggressive or submissive
- Being emotional
- Appearing disorganized and lacking control of your work
- Giving in without attempting to renegotiate

Perfectionism and Procrastination

Whether you spend too long on a project, or you simply delay starting it, both these faults can make major inroads into your time.

Don't Miss Your Deadlines

It is possible to finish a project on time and still be late – if you don't realize that it's finished! Perfectionism is a subtle barrier: you are doing a job, and doing it well, but somehow you're never satisfied and keep on making changes. Some of the brightest people suffer the most from perfectionism – they just don't know when to stop.

Let's suppose you are writing an article for a journal. Halfway through, you think of a better way to structure it, so you start over. Then you see a better way, and so on. Before you know it, the deadline is upon you and the article isn't ready, although it would have been if you had been satisfied sooner.

CASE study: Controlling Perfectionism

Lara and her husband loved socializing and having people over. Lara's problem was that she was finding it increasingly difficult to enjoy her own parties. She realized that she spent so much time planning and arranging the party that when it finally arrived, she was too tired to have a good time.

Lara's husband solved her problem. On the day of the party, he insisted that she stop what she was doing at 5 p.m., take a shower, and come out for a drive with him. Initially she found it difficult, but gradually Lara began to relax.

• *Lara's husband realized that her desire to be a perfect hostess had led her to prepare unnecessarily complicated dishes and to check and recheck arrangements, all of which proved exhausting.*

• *By setting a deadline, he limited the amount of time that Lara could spend preparing, which meant she scaled back and did only what was necessary. As a result Lara was more relaxed, her guests enjoyed her company, and she started to enjoy her own parties again; the details were less important than a good time.*

think
SMART

!

**Try leaving less important jobs to the last minute –
it will force you to control your perfectionist streak.**

This can be a great way of controlling time spent on a job –
with a fixed deadline, you have to do the job as well as
possible within the time available. Avoid trying this with an
important job, though – it could backfire if something goes
unexpectedly wrong.

To put a task in perspective, step back for a moment and
ask yourself how much difference a little more effort
is really going to make, and whether continuing with the
job will force you to take time away from another
important activity. The answer to this second question
should deter you from allowing tasks to expand
unnecessarily. Identify the tasks you tend to linger on, and
set clear deadlines on them. Schedule other tasks straight
after these, so that you have to move on.

Think About the Consequences

Another way to look at this is to analyze the consequences
of getting the job slightly wrong. If you are arranging
supper with an old friend, it doesn't make sense to spend
a long time writing an e-mail invitation – the consequences
of making a spelling mistake are negligible. Equally, if you
are preparing a routine presentation to your team, then –
unless you make a monumental error – the situation is
recoverable. In routine situations such as these, you should
aim for something that is "good enough". On the other
hand, if people's lives depend on
your work, it is vital that you do
the job properly – and yes, by all
means double-check, and even
triple-check it, if necessary.

> **Never let yesterday
> use up today.**
> Richard H. Nelson

Face Up to Procrastination

Putting something off – even when we know it must be done eventually – is the greatest trap of all. We all know this, and yet we all continue to fall into the trap and it costs us time and energy. There are many reasons why we put off doing a task:

- Sometimes we find it overwhelming – it seems too complex or too vast.
- Sometimes we are not equipped to deal with it.
- Sometimes it is too boring to engage upon or we think it is too unpleasant.
- Sometimes we simply know that we do not want to do it.

If you feel overwhelmed, pick a small task and just get started

Punishing yourself for your procrastination just compounds the problem, so accept that it is a fact of life, shrug off the guilt, and try to tackle the root-cause of the problem. Here are a few tools to help you overcome the initial inertia.

The Swiss-Cheese Technique

If you feel that a task is too complex or time-consuming, don't push yourself into tackling the task head-on. Instead, pick up a small "instant task" related to the main project – something that can be done quickly and easily – and do it. Follow this with another task, and another, and you will effectively eat away at the project. It is, to borrow an analogy from time-management expert Alan Lakein, like poking holes in a cheese: the more holes you make, the more you will get involved with the project.

The same technique can be used to tackle unpleasant tasks. Find a small five-minute activity related to the project. Give yourself permission to quit after five minutes,

The secret of getting ahead, is getting started.

Sally Berger

but not before – after all, it can't be that unbearable. And a series of five-minute teasers might make you realize that the task isn't quite as bad as you had expected.

The Baby-Steps Method

Whereas the Swiss Cheese technique involves identifying a single small task, the Baby-Steps method renders an overwhelming task manageable by breaking it into a series of bite-sized tasks. Although structuring your project as a chain of small, specific steps requires detailed planning, it usually pays dividends.

Plan your campaign on the calendar – working back from an end date – and plot the sub-tasks you will need to do. The project will automatically become more manageable – instead of focusing on the entire "overwhelming" task, you are dealing with simpler sub-tasks. Try planning a series of small rewards for each step accomplished.

Brick by Brick Even the most complex project is more manageable if broken into a series of small tasks. Like building a wall, focus on laying each brick – before you know it, the whole project will be complete.

Reinforcement Techniques

Once you have set your goal and formulated a plan to achieve it, positive reinforcement techniques can motivate you and ensure that you stay on course.

→ Link up with others who have similar priorities and goals. This may mean like-minded friends, or more structured support groups. It is inspiring to know that others share a similar vision – and seeing others making progress jolts you into action, too.

→ Surround yourself with positive reminders and reinforcing statements. The power of positive suggestion is considerable.

→ Make a commitment to someone. Get a significant other to be your watchdog, and report to him or her. You could even write out a formal contract. When you know you are accountable to someone, you tend to move faster.

→ Reward yourself: bribes work, so break up your plan into bite-sized goals and set up a series of small rewards for each step.

→ Keep a note of your progress. Ticking off completed tasks as you do them will remind you how far you have already come and give you the confidence and the momentum to continue.

→ Give yourself a break. Once you have made a start on a difficult task, the temptation can be to press on regardless. But taking regular, guilt-free breaks will help you avoid burnout.

Effective Ways to Prevent Procrastination

HIGH IMPACT

- Breaking large, intimidating tasks down into small, achievable ones
- Identifying and then doing one small action after another
- Doing unpleasant tasks at your most productive time of day
- Rewarding yourself afterwards with something you enjoy

NEGATIVE IMPACT

- Setting yourself up to tackle large tasks, all in one go
- Worrying too much about doing tasks in the most efficient order – unless it's necessary
- Leaving unpleasant tasks until the end of the day, when you are tired and low in willpower

CASE study: Overcoming Procrastination

Lee had been planning a holiday in Goa for quite some time, but somehow she just couldn't get around to it. She decided to make it a priority, and wrote "GO GOA" on her bulletin boards at home and at the office. She placed the travel brochures in prominent positions on the coffee table, bought a new bikini, and blocked out holiday dates in her calendar. And the trip to Goa finally did materialize.

• By surrounding herself with reinforcing statements, Lee began to view the trip as a real possibility rather than a vague dream. The reminders also meant that she could no longer put the holiday to the back of her mind and focus on more immediate priorities.

• The brochures helped Lee to focus on the outcome – the holiday itself – rather than the steps required to get there.

Don't Overplan Your Project

Perhaps your reluctance to start a project is due to the fact that you don't know enough about it. The obvious starting point is to gather the relevant information, but don't get sucked into "the knowing-doing gap". This is when you continue collecting knowledge, or information, about a project but never actually get around to doing it. You are falling into the knowing-doing gap when you start believing:
• that knowing about something is sufficient for success
• that planning and talking about things is the same as action
• that making a decision is the same as taking action.
Shake yourself out of it, and tell yourself that – ready or not – you will start the project on a specific date. The chances are that you have done enough preparation.

Focus On the Outcome

Perhaps you keep putting off a particular task because you don't like doing it. If you cannot delegate it, then evaluate what you stand to lose if you either delay it or simply do not do it. Then decide whether you are willing to take the consequences: assess the benefits of doing it along with the unpleasantness that will result from not doing it.

Understand Your Energy Cycles

We all have natural energy cycles that ebb and flow during the course of a day. These ups and downs can have a profound impact on our effectiveness.

Plot Your Energy Curve

Are you aware of your energy cycles? Do you perform best in the morning or the afternoon? When are your low spots? A good way to find out is by using the model below and plotting your energy throughout the day. Once you feel fully functional in the morning, draw a dot on the chart to represent your energy levels. Set an alarm to go off every hour and, every time it beeps, place a corresponding dot on the chart. Do this for several days.

Join up the dots: your peak productivity zone is where the curve rises above the 75 per cent energy level. Everything below the 25 per cent level is your down time. Try to schedule your most complex, critical, and highest-paying jobs in the peak productivity time zone: you will achieve faster, higher-quality results.

Productivity Zones

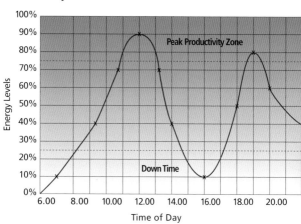

Energy Cycles Plot the daily fluctuations in your energy levels. If you can identify when you feel most energetic, you will know the best time to schedule important tasks.

Find Your Energy Boosters

You can't always control when you do certain tasks, and some are bound to fall in your down time. This is where energy boosters are useful.

The best time-managers know which activities give them a boost when their energy is flagging. They use this knowledge when faced with a demanding task at a time when they feel low. Think about what energizes you and then use this booster to give you an instant recharge when needed. Sometimes, just a change of pace will raise your energy levels. Different things work for different people, but you might like to try the following:

→ **Get moving** If your brain feels in need of a break, get up and do something that requires you to move around and use your muscles.

Try to pinpoint what makes you feel more energetic

→ **Refuel** Eat a snack, or drink a cup of coffee. This will give you the energy you need, or stimulate you to complete the task. Quick release carbohydrates (such as energy bars) give an immediate boost, but can later leave you feeling drained. Slower-release carbohydrates (such as bread) take longer to act, but will sustain you for a longer period.

→ **Listen to music** Take a few minutes to switch off and listen to music that you find relaxing. Alternatively, listen to music that you find inspirational, exciting, and motivating.

→ **Have a chat** Talking to your co-workers can lift your mood and give you the break you need to focus on your work.

→ **Take a break** Most people tend to underestimate the energy boost that a simple break can give – it revitalizes you. Take at least three five-minute breaks each day. Use these short breaks to simply sit back and do nothing, or go for a short walk. Soon you will realize that these short periods of relaxation vastly recharge your energy levels.

Summary: Ending Wasted Time

Plan of Action

Our aim in this chapter has been to work out why some, or all, projects are not proceeding as they should. Assuming that the Next Action Organizer and the support systems that enable this to function are properly in place and working for you, we've pinned the problem down to time-wasters. These can be other people's interruptions or our own ways of wasting time.

Are you distracted by frequent interruptions?

Do you tend to procrastinate and put tasks off?

Do you have systems in place to organize your work?

YES →

Do you find it hard to finish tasks?

NO ↓

Return to Chapter Two and put in place the Action Programme

Handle Perfectionism

Be realistic about what you can achieve

Set yourself deadlines

Minimize Interruptions

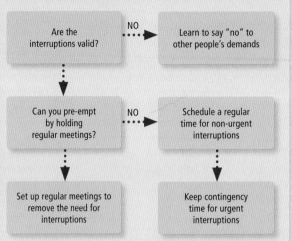

Are the interruptions valid? — **NO** → Learn to say "no" to other people's demands

Can you pre-empt by holding regular meetings? — **NO** → Schedule a regular time for non-urgent interruptions

Set up regular meetings to remove the need for interruptions

Keep contingency time for urgent interruptions

Face up to Procrastination

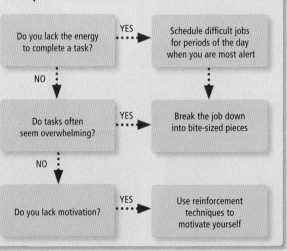

Do you lack the energy to complete a task? — **YES** → Schedule difficult jobs for periods of the day when you are most alert

NO

Do tasks often seem overwhelming? — **YES** → Break the job down into bite-sized pieces

NO

Do you lack motivation? — **YES** → Use reinforcement techniques to motivate yourself

Time is Money

Whether interruptions, perfectionism, or procrastination hold you back, knowing just how much every wasted minute costs will help you to blast through the barrier.

Calculate the Value of Your Time

Once you know the value of your time, you will tend to use it more effectively – having a proper appreciation of the value of your time is an essential step in good time management. If you are working for yourself, for example, you should have an idea of how much income you want to earn. Working these figures back to an hourly rate will give you a good idea of the value of your time. If you're employed by someone else, run through the following calculation to estimate the value of your time.

Increasing Value If your employer has invested money training you, or if you've spent time or money gaining skills for yourself, this increases your value. Don't waste it on tasks that have a lower value than your time.

> **You don't get paid for the hour, you get paid for the work that you bring to the hour.**
> Jim Rohn

Add together the approximate figures for:

- Your salary and benefits
- Your employer's payroll tax (which can be around 12.5 per cent of your salary)
- A contribution for rent, equipment, heating, and so on (say 10 per cent of your salary and benefits)
- A contribution for overheads and services (say 40 per cent of your salary and benefits)
- Profit expected (use a value of 50 per cent of all the above costs added together).

> **Eliminate or delegate tasks that have a lower value than your time**

Once you have the total cost, calculate how many days that you work each year. This is probably the total number of possible working days (52 x 5) minus holiday leave, public holidays, training, and any days lost through illness.

Know Your Value

Dividing the total cost by the number of working days gives you the value of your day; dividing this by the number of hours that you work daily gives your hourly rate. You may be surprised by the high value of your time! This figure shows you the average value you should aim to deliver with your time if you intend to be a satisfactory performer. If you want to be a high achiever, you should aim to offer substantially better value than "average".

Place a rough value on each tasks you do. Where possible, focus on tasks that have a value greater than the calculated value of your time, and delegate or outsource the rest. When you find that your time is being wasted, remind yourself that your time is money – and you now know how much money. This will help to spur you on.

Delegate Efficiently

4

There is a limit to the amount of work you can do yourself – you have to be able to free yourself from the routine tasks that consume your time and energy so that you can focus on higher-priority, higher-return jobs. The key to achieving this freedom is delegation. Effective delegation means getting things done the right way, at the right time, by the right people. This chapter teaches you:

- What to delegate and how to overcome any reluctance to delegate
- How to select the right person for the job, define the delegated task clearly, and provide essential feedback and support
- What checks you need to ensure that tasks are completed on time and to standard.

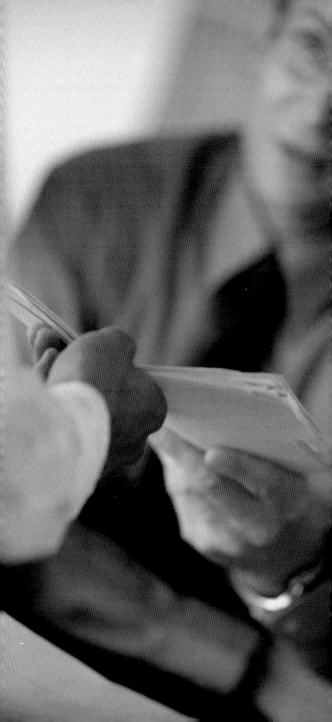

Don't Hold Back

Delegation is a vital tool in management, so why are we often reluctant to redistribute our workload to others, even when our job requires us to do so?

Use Your Team

Effective delegating is essential, especially if you are a manager. Your team has more collective time, energy, and, in some cases, more knowledge for these tasks than you do. Too often, however, something holds us back.

> **Delegation leaves you free to focus on the jobs that need you most**

"No Problem: I Can Manage This, Too"

The desire to do it all yourself usually stems from a need to feel indispensable. In fact, your own importance would be increased if you were able to focus personally on those activities that could not be done by others.

Often, too, you are so comfortable doing one particular type of task that you do not want to delegate it. The danger with staying inside your "comfort zone" is that you will fail to stretch yourself to develop the new skills and capabilities that you need to further your career.

"It's Quicker and Easier if I Do It Myself"

People under pressure often prefer to do a job themselves rather than take the time to explain the task to someone else and then monitor their progress. Yet time spent delegating is an investment – especially if the task is one that will be regularly repeated in the future. Even one-off tasks can help to develop team members.

"I Don't Want to Dump it on Others"

This one arises out of misguided benevolence. You need to recognize that your time is valuable and should not be spent on routine work that others could do. Work that is dull for you may be challenging for people with less

experience and, anyway, people aren't paid to have fun – they are paid to get the job done.

Learn to Delegate Routine tasks can and should be delegated in order to free up time for high-level tasks. Remember that work that is dull for you may be much more stimulating for people with less experience

"They Can't Manage It"

Sometimes, a lack of confidence in others is justified, but often it is not. It usually pays big dividends to invest a little time in training: as well as saving time, you are also building your teams' skills and confidence. If you really don't have people to whom you can delegate, that situation needs to be remedied.

TIP Do not make yourself too indispensable – indispensable people can't be promoted. It is easier to move you up once you've groomed your successor.

Write an Activity Delegation Log

The first step towards effective delegation is to identify the tasks and projects in which you are involved that could, potentially, be partly or wholly delegated.

Learn to Delegate More

The process of analyzing your workload in this way enables you to see whether you are delegating effectively and also helps you to prepare delegation strategies for major projects. If you are following the **Next Action Organizer** that we discussed in the earlier chapters, you should be delegating at least some of the jobs that come your way – but are you managing to achieve full delegation? The Activity Delegation Log will help you to find out.

Using the template below as a guide, list at least ten activities that take from 1–12 hours of your time each week (take a look at those actions on the **Action Programme** you created in Chapter Two). Estimate the total time you spend each week on each activity, and then decide whether you can delegate that activity fully, partially, or not at all. If you are not sure, check the table above. Once you have completed your log, you will

The Activity Delegation Log

Major Activities w/c 16 Jan	Time Spent	Could I have Delegated?		
		Fully	Partially	Not at all
Preparing team progress reports	4hrs	✓		
Selecting new customer service supervisor	3½ hrs			✓
Handling RMC product quality problems	3 hrs		✓	
Materials analysis for Gordondale product	2½ hrs	✓		

Analyze Your Tasks A Delegation Log helps you take a step back, analyze how well you delegate Activities, and identify those you should delegate in the future.

Delegation Criteria

DELEGATE

- Routine tasks
- Tasks that can be done better by other people
- Tasks that would benefit from other people's specialist skills
- Tasks that develop team members
- Tasks that test team members

DO NOT DELEGATE

- Tasks that are emergencies and require your skill or judgement
- Tasks that require unofficial action
- Tasks that involve monitoring, evaluating, and rewarding team members
- Tasks that concern discipline

---

probably find that you could be delegating many more tasks than you realized – and freeing up a significant amount of your time in the process.

Delegate Projects

The Activity Delegation Log will have revealed those individual tasks and actions that you may be able to delegate. The second part of this method involves planning delegation strategies for major projects. The best place to start this is in the Project Catalogue section of your **Action Programme**.

Look at each project as a whole and break it down into specific tasks. Using the delegation criteria mentioned above, decide which tasks only you can do. Then, determine the tasks that can be given to other people. You will probably find recurring or routine items, such as monthly reports, that can be equally well-handled by someone else. Delegate accordingly.

The skills needed to schedule and manage complex projects are significant – for very large projects, project management is a discipline and profession in its own right, and you may benefit from bringing in the expertise of a professional project manager.

Never tell people how to do things. Tell them what to do and they will surprise you with their ingenuity

General George S. Patton Jr.

Find the Right Person for the Job

How do you decide which job to assign to which person in your team? Sometimes the answer is obvious, but often this extremely important decision is a difficult one.

Develop and Enhance People's Skills

You should consider whether delegation enhances an employee's growth. Perhaps a member of your team has done part of this task before, but not all of it. Perhaps the time has come to stretch that team member and widen his or her experience. One useful approach is to delegate the task to the most junior organizational level required for its performance. This frees people at higher levels to carry out tasks more suited to their experience, while those at lower levels get a chance to learn skills and gain confidence.

Delegate tasks to the lowest organizational level suitable for the job

Use People's Knowledge and Experience

A person's talents must be taken into account when assigning a job. Certain jobs will fall within the remit of individuals who already have some knowledge of the task in hand, and may have a proven track record. Always keep a close eye on the successful completion of the task. For urgent, important, or high-visibility jobs, choose people with a proven capability: you need to be confident that the tasks will be completed successfully. Lower-profile, non-urgent tasks are useful for developing people's abilities. Try to offer as many such opportunities as possible.

Organize People's Workloads

Make sure you consider the current workload of the person to whom you are assigning the task. The most suitable person may already be too busy. If he or she really is the right person for the job, you may have to renegotiate other tasks on their list.

Assign Delegated Tasks

How do you decide which job to assign to which person on your team? Consider the example of Helen, a project manager. Helen has a product launch coming up and has several tasks to delegate: invitations to be sent out, a presentation to be researched and written, and launch details to be co-ordinated. She can delegate these tasks to the people in her team: Traci, the secretary; Katie, the research assistant; and Andres and Nuria, both marketing executives.

Invitations Several people need to be telephoned and invited. It makes sense to assign the job to Traci. She stands at the lowest organizational level, but is fully qualified to handle the job. The other members of the team will be better employed doing other jobs.

Research Katie is the obvious choice to take on the task of researching for the presentation. Until now, Helen has only entrusted Katie with data collection, while she writes the presentations. Helen feels that Katie is now ready to do this too, and wants her to develop her skills.

Co-ordination
Co-ordinating the details of the launch party is beyond Traci's scope. Helen wants to assign it to either Nuria or Andres, since both have previous experience of this type of task. However, Nuria is busy with another project, whereas Andres has more free time and is therefore more motivated. Helen delegates the job to Andres.

Delegate Fully and Clearly

People take better care of things they own. When you delegate a task, assign responsibility specifically to the person to whom you are delegating the task.

Cover All the Elements

Ensure that both you and the person to whom you are delegating have a clear understanding of what is involved. Ask the team member to repeat back to you their understanding of the job so that you can double-check this. Make certain that the person to whom you are delegating clearly understands:

- What the task is and why it needs to be done
- When you expect it to be completed
- The specific goals you expect him or her to achieve
- The person to whom he or she is responsible
- The extent of his or her authority to make decisions
- What problems need to be referred back to you
- What the progress-reporting mechanisms are
- The check points at which you will review progress
- The information and support you are willing to provide
- What resources will be available.

TECHNIQUES *to practise*

Use the following set of delegating skills to ensure that you get what is expected, particularly when delegating complex, costly, or time-critical projects
It is all too easy for small misunderstandings early on in a project to snowball into major problems as the project progresses. To avoid this occurring:

- Ensure that you get a detailed description of what will be delivered early on in the project, and take the time to check this through thoroughly.
- Check that any unknowns or risks related to the project are understood and managed.
- Inspect the progress and the quality of the delegated work at pre-agreed times.

Delegation Worksheet

Task:	*Send new product brochures to last year's Q4 clients*
Purpose & Context:	*To let clients who bought from us at the end of last year know about our latest product range, so that they'll upgrade to our new generation products.*
Completion Date	*30 June*
Specific Goals:	• *Cleaned database* • *High-quality delivery*
Check Points & Reporting:	• *On completion of database cleaning with list of cleaned names and addresses: by 14 June* • *With proposed cover letter and mock-up of what the client will receive: by 21 June* • *Completed mailshot with unsealed envelopes, but otherwise ready to dispatch: by 25 June*
Support and Resources:	*Nicki Jackowska will help you make the database-cleaning phone calls and with mailshot packaging. Will need to book high-volume printer well in advance. Any problems or questions, refer back.*

Write it Down If you are delegating a large or complex task, a worksheet structured on these lines helps both parties to understand clearly what is expected. Don't fill it in yourself, though; get the person to whom you are delegating to do it.

If the task you are delegating is complex, ensure that the delegated person takes notes. Research shows that people typically hold only about six items of information in their short-term memories – if you exceed that limit, or if the person to whom you are delegating has other information to remember, the instructions may be forgotten. For large tasks, get the person to whom you are delegating to put together a delegation worksheet such as the one above.

> **The best executive is the one who has sense enough to pick good men... and self-restraint enough to keep from meddling with them while they do it.**
>
> Theodore Roosevelt

Monitor the Work

Even after you assign the right job to the right person, you still have to ensure that it gets done accurately and on time. Set up an effective and regular monitoring system so that you are able to follow up on progress. Don't be embarrassed about monitoring people – they expect it, and will probably welcome your interest.

Review Progress Regularly

When it comes to monitoring progress, don't wait for the deadline – it may be too late by then. Instead, schedule regular appointments to review all those tasks that you have delegated. Keep a list of them on your **Action Programme**, and write down the agreed check-in points. Quick meetings at pre-designated times will help you to ensure that everything is on track, and you will be able to nip potential problems in the bud.

5 minute FIX

If you are too busy to explain and monitor the delegated task yourself, why not delegate this role too?

Pick a team member who you feel is too experienced or too busy to do the original task, but who has the knowledge and ability to monitor a more junior team member. Take five minutes to explain to what you want, and then leave him or her to handle the briefing and monitoring process.

Exchange Information

As well as being an excellent way of keeping you up-to-date on the work, progress reviews also provide an invaluable opportunity for an exchange of information between you and your team members. Use each review as a platform to communicate with your team member and to seek his or her feedback on the assignment. Remember

TIP Always encourage your team members to approach you if they feel that they might have a problem completing the task.

Avoid Interference

It is often difficult to know where to draw the line between monitoring progress closely enough to ensure that the task is completed correctly and on schedule, and avoiding interference. The trick here is to agree a sensible report-back frequency.

→ If your checkpoints are too close together, then too much time will be taken up in checkpoint meetings and in preparation for them, so little progress will be made in between them.

→ If checkpoints are too far apart, then you won't have time to take corrective action if things are going astray.

In between checkpoints, make sure that you keep in touch with team members and are available to help them if they ask for help. Otherwise, let them get on with the job. Get more closely involved only if things start going wrong.

that part of your role at these meetings is to coach your team member on any issues that he or she is already facing, or will face at the next stage. You should also make sure that you clear any unnecessary obstacles out of their way, so that the team member can perform effectively.

Identify Potential Problems

If you feel a project might run into problems, always keep a closer-than-usual eye on it, and be aware that you may need to make contingency plans if things don't run on course. Realistically, you can expect that work will not always be finished to your complete satisfaction, particularly when delegating to someone for the first time.

Monitoring delegated work is a bit like going to the dentist for regular check-ups. The idea is to detect problems before they have a chance to become serious, and to take steps to put things right, as early as possible.

Summary: Delegating Effectively

Effective delegation is an important time-saving art that will free up your time for higher-value tasks. Being able to delegate successfully means passing the right tasks to the right people, making sure that the task is clearly defined and fully understood, and then monitoring the progress of that work to a satisfactory conclusion.

Plan of Action

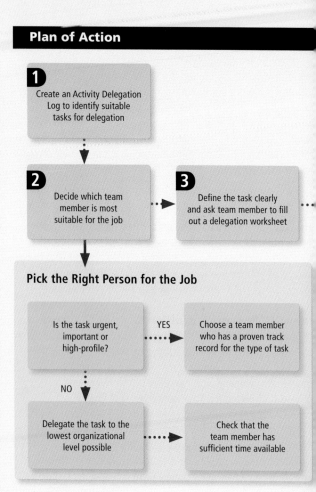

1 Create an Activity Delegation Log to identify suitable tasks for delegation

2 Decide which team member is most suitable for the job

3 Define the task clearly and ask team member to fill out a delegation worksheet

Pick the Right Person for the Job

Is the task urgent, important or high-profile?

YES → Choose a team member who has a proven track record for the type of task

NO ↓

Delegate the task to the lowest organizational level possible → Check that the team member has sufficient time available

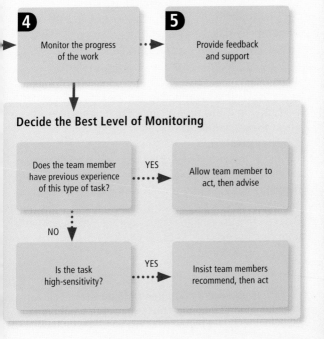

4
Monitor the progress of the work

5
Provide feedback and support

Decide the Best Level of Monitoring

Does the team member have previous experience of this type of task? — **YES** → Allow team member to act, then advise

NO

Is the task high-sensitivity? — **YES** → Insist team members recommend, then act

Avoid Problems and Pitfalls

Delegation sounds straightforward, but it can be hard to do well. It takes a concerted effort to avoid slipping into bad habits, and there are also numerous pitfalls that can undermine your best efforts.

Achieve the Right Balance

One of the biggest risks of delegating is that the person to whom you have delegated a job might make a major error. That's why you must make sure that any mistakes remain affordable. The process of monitoring delegated work is a fine balancing act. On the one hand, you want to give your team member the freedom and responsibility to get on with the job in their own way, without you breathing down his or her neck. But at the same time, you can't afford to sit back and allow a delicate project to go badly off the rails. It is therefore vital that you establish a control mechanism to ensure that any mistakes stay within limits, while also giving team members as much space as possible to do things the way they want to. After all, people will only have a chance to develop new ways of doing things, and perhaps even improve on the old ways, if you let them.

> **Risk depends on the nature of the task, and on the team member's skills**

One of the real joys of delegation is when you receive an end-product that, because it's been created using team members' full creativity, is even better than the one that you had originally had in mind. However, one of the things that can most severely damage your reputation is when an important project fails because you have not given it close enough supervision.

TIP If you are a manager, pass on the credit for success and absorb the consequences of failure.

Assess Your Risk

There are two important variables determining the degree of freedom that you can afford the other person – the sensitivity of the project, and the reliability of the person to whom you have delegated the work.

The more critical the task, the more cautious you need to be about extending too much freedom. The more experienced and reliable the person, the more freedom you can give. Authors Kenneth Blanchard, William Oncken Jr, and Hal Burrows, in their book *The One Minute Manager Meets the Monkey*, suggest two basic strategies for dealing appropriately with this risk:

→ **Act and then Advise:** Encourage team members to employ this strategy if a task is routine or relatively low-risk, or you know that the person to whom you have delegated the work is fully competent and can handle the task successfully on their own. Leave your team member to do the job and also resolve matters, but make sure they inform you later about the action they have taken.

→ **Recommend and then Act:** If a task is particularly sensitive then, regardless of capability, you will want the team member to check with you before acting. Ask for a recommendation, which, pending your approval, he or she can then implement. This provides insurance in situations where there's a reasonable risk that the person might make an unaffordable mistake, if unsupervised. The same strategy should be applied when a team member is handling a task for the first time.

Delegation Strategies

ACT, THEN ADVISE	RECOMMEND, THEN ACT
• Routine tasks	• One-off tasks
• Low-sensitivity tasks	• High-sensitivity tasks
• Experienced team members	• Inexperienced team members

Avoid Reverse Delegation

Managers often find themselves caught in a situation where, instead of delegating work to their employees, they are actually taking on the employees' responsibilities. Reverse delegation happens subtly. Your team member walks in and says, "Boss, we have a problem". He or she describes the problem, and you respond by saying, "I'll look into it". With this one statement you have taken on the burden, instead of encouraging the team member to retain ownership by suggesting solutions to the problem. Whether you were short on time, thought the person was incompetent, or are simply in the habit of doing things yourself, the result is the same: your subordinate has just parked the problem at your door and walked away from it.

Clarify the Ground Rules

By applying what you have learnt in the earlier chapters, you should be able to protect yourself against reverse

CASE study: Solving Reverse Delegation

Rashid had just been promoted to customer services manager as a result of his success at solving clients' problems. However, he was struggling to manage his new workload, because his staff constantly passed on "problem" calls from clients; in fact, callers were stacked up, waiting. Realizing this couldn't go on, Rashid started asking team members how they would handle a call, whenever they tried putting someone through to him. If they gave an inappropriate answer, he dealt with the caller, but he discussed the solution at the next day's team meeting. Soon, things were back under control.

• *Rashid was letting people pass on problems that they could solve themselves. By pushing people to come up with solutions, he cleared time in his own schedule.*
• *His actions pushed people to think for themselves, and by discussing the more complicated cases at team meetings, his staff learned to solve some of these more difficult problems for themselves, which increased customer satisfaction.*

delegation. But, if not, you will have to set things straight. You are there to supervise your staff, not to do their job for them. Next time someone approaches you with a problem, guide him or her in handling it, but do not take on the burden of doing it yourself.

Ask for "The Next Move"

Get your team members into the habit of offering solutions to their problems. These may not be perfect, but by giving you suggestions to work with, you will probably then be in a stronger position to help them. You will also encourage ownership by encouraging team members to find their own solutions to problems that arise.

Start fostering the expectation that they must always contribute thoughtful recommendations for the "next moves" to be made on any given situation. Your team members will then get into the habit of doing preparation work before coming to you – saving both their time and yours. This approach also has the important advantage of breaking a project into manageable, bite-sized pieces. While people can often feel intimidated by the size and apparent complexity of a large problem, the process of breaking it down into smaller pieces (or even just the right "next move") can often help them to move forward with the problem and eventually solve it.

5 minute FIX

If you've been caught by reverse delegation, problems can quickly build up and projects may stall.

Use this technique to break the blockage down quickly:

- List the problems creating the blockage.

- Ask each person who reverse-delegated to you to prepare recommendations.

- If they cannot solve the problem, find someone who can, and ask them for recommendations.

TIP While you must be firm with people to avoid reverse delegation, be alert if they are struggling – part of a manager's job is to coach and support.

Provide Feedback and Support

Delegation isn't just a matter of telling someone else what to do. You still have a responsibility to that person to provide the necessary support and guidance.

Make Time for Communication

Instead of leaving your team members to their own devices and waiting for them to bring their problems to you, remember to schedule appointments with them at your convenience – as agreed when you delegated the task. In this way they can keep you informed on progress, and you will have a chance to offer advice. You will also discover that when someone knows that you plan to meet on a specific date, he or she is more likely to complete work in a timely manner and solve any problems before the scheduled appointment.

Encourage Communication By adopting a relaxed, open, and alert posture, you will encourage the team member you are monitoring to share their concerns and admit any errors.

Help with Personal Development

When you offer support, learn to consider it in its widest possible context. It's easy to think about giving support in a caring sense, where you help someone adjust to difficult circumstances. But it involves much more:

→ Helping team members gain the skills and knowledge they need to do their job properly. Consider whether they would benefit best from informal mentoring, coaching, or training courses.

→ Removing any barriers to progress by intervening and asking the relevant people to clear a path for your staff.

→ Helping people work effectively as a team: mentoring, socializing, and celebrating successes can all foster team spirit.

Offer Support

If you have delegated a job, make sure that the person concerned has the authority to access necessary resources, and check that he or she knows how to locate them. Clear away potential obstacles and make sure that the person is briefed on any awkward matters concerning politics or protocol. Do not leave the person to inform your own peers of his or her new responsibilities. If the task is important and sufficiently high profile, then inform your own boss – and anyone else who needs to know.

Motivate Your Team Members

It is important to let the person know how they are doing, and whether they have achieved their aims. If they have accomplished their goal, give them praise – praise is a powerful motivating force. If they did not achieve their goal, review their actions to identify what went wrong, deal with any problems, and offer encouragement. Identify any faults and errors, but give plenty of credit where it is due. This will help them do a better job in the future.

Make Use of Leverage

Where we get to in life often depends on the "power" that we can exert. However hard we work, we can only exert a certain amount of power on our own. People who move beyond this do so with specialist knowledge, with other people's help, or by using technology. These types of leverage are essential if you want to raise the results bar. In this chapter, we look at:

• The concept of leverage and the ways in which you can harness the available resources to help you make the most of your time

• The use of knowledge, education, and technology to give yourself the edge

• The leverage of other people's time.

The Concept of Leverage

Used in the right way, leverage can catapult your time-management efforts into an different orbit, helping you to get far more done with only a little more effort.

Learn to Achieve More

Like a mechanical lever, leverage in business and time management helps you use your strength more effectively. However hard you work, you can do only so much with your time without using leverage skills, which means that your career will stall. To move beyond this point, you need to learn to harness knowledge, technology, money, and other people's time – this is the only way to achieve results in excess of the time that you put in.

Use What You Have

Leverage is about taking full advantage of the available resources – your own and other people's – to optimize your performance and get the most from your time. We've already discussed delegation, one of the first forms of leverage most people come across. However, we shall now look at a range of other sources of leverage, all of which can help you to achieve much more with your time.

think SMART

To appreciate the advantages that leverage can bring to almost any area of life, consider the contrast between a high jumper and a pole vaulter.

Unaided, an Olympic high jumper can clear the bar at over two metres – but, with the aid of a pole, the vaulter can clear almost six metres! This isn't because he's a better athlete – it's because he is using the pole as leverage. Apply this lesson to your own life and work: instead of a pole, use money, knowledge, or technology to maximize your efficiency, increase the return on your time, and push ahead of your competitors.

Increase Your Power Using the leverage of a jack, you can easily raise a heavy car – an almost impossible feat without a lever. In time management, levers such as money, technology, and education provide similar gains.

> **If I have seen further, it is by standing on the shoulders of giants.**
>
> Sir Isaac Newton

The Use of Time

In essence, this book is about time leverage – using your time efficiently and effectively to get the greatest possible value from it. To do this, you should be focused on the goals that are truly important to you, and you should also know how to avoid distractions. If you have followed the tips and suggestions in this book so far, you should be in full control of your workload, and have a comfortable and achievable schedule. You will have an efficient support system that keeps you in control, and you should be well on your way to effective delegation of large parts of your workload to other people.

Harness Education and Technology

The importance of education is obvious. If you know what you are trying to do and know how to do it, then you are considerably more effective. In the same way, technology has huge potential to increase productivity.

The Costly Learning Curve

Further education can seem daunting, particularly if you have already embarked on a career. But, if you don't know how to do something, finding out through trial and error can take a long time. The ups and downs of the learning process can also affect on your credibility. Who wants to be operated on by surgeons, or fly with pilots who are working it out as they go? And even when you have worked out a viable solution, you will never be confident that it is the best one.

If you're serious about a goal, the time spent learning will be time well spent

Work More Effectively

Unfortunately, it's just too easy to blunder into an area without thinking about the knowledge you need. If you do this, you risk wasting huge amounts of time and can end up performing in a way that will be best described as mediocre. You also risk seeing younger but better-educated people sprint past you, simply because they have learned the right answers rather than worked them out slowly by experience. They will also have acquired the language and the tools to continue to make progress.

Target Your Needs

Earlier on, you identified your life goals and the things you want to achieve. Now, for each of the goals, assume an outsider's perspective and ask yourself what skills and education are needed for the efficient and successful attainment of those goals. There will undoubtedly be many instances where you simply don't have the knowledge, so

Develop Support Networks

A powerful side-effect of getting the best education you can is that you plug into support mechanisms and professional networks used by people with similar goals. This provides a powerful leverage of experience and assistance, and everything becomes easier. There are plenty of ways to develop a support network:

→ Professional bodies often provide training and support and may organize seminars and events.

→ Join a relevant club, society, or support group.

→ Attend training courses or take a university degree in your relevant subject, and network with fellow students.

→ Visit trade or consumer shows, and subscribe to magazines serving your area of interest.

→ Join a relevant on-line community or forum.

make sure you take the appropriate courses and acquire the knowledge needed to reach these goals. Aim for the best education and training you can get. This could take a long time, but if you are serious about achieving your goals, it won't be time wasted.

Use Education in Your Personal Life

Many of the same arguments apply to entering any new field, including personal interests and pastimes. Why waste time finding out what other people already know and can easily pass on to you? For example, working out how to snowboard could take days of experiments and could cost a broken wrist, whereas a one-day course will soon have you up and enjoying the experience safely.

TIP **Find out which institutions are best respected in the area of learning you are interested in; the most respected institutions deliver the highest leverage.**

Use Technology

There are countless examples of companies that would have been, at most, a regional success 20 years ago, but which have made use of technology to become international household names serving a world-wide market. Even on a much smaller scale, databases, e-mail, standard letters, spreadsheets, and vertical market software applications offer huge improvements in productivity, speed, and accuracy of service.

Make the Right Choice

Think about the work you do now, and the work that you will need to do, to achieve your goals. Are parts of it repetitive, and could these be automated? Are there parts that could be speeded up?

5 minute FIX

If you don't already use them, take five minutes to look up and learn your computer's most common keyboard shortcuts.

On a PC, use Ctrl+C and Ctrl+V to copy and paste text, and Ctrl+Z to undo mistakes. Other functions that take a few minutes to learn or set up but can save hours of repetition include:

- Macros, to automate repetitive tasks

- Templates, for creating common document formats

- MSWord Autocorrect, to automate frequently repeated text entry and make common corrections automatically.

Could investment in the right technology improve the quality of your product? Or could you get much greater impact by spending a little money on technology and investing time in learning how to use it? If you feel unsure about an investment, ask yourself three crucial questions:

- Do I need this product?
- Does the technology give me an edge?
- Will I use the features that I am paying for?

Of course, you can spend a huge amount of time and money on technology and this can be a great source of procrastination – but a sensible, well-focused investment can give tremendous leverage and yield huge returns.

Choose Technology to Suit Your Needs

Having the latest or most sophisticated technology is only useful in so far as it serves your needs. Take the example of Reva (a housewife), her husband Cecil (a management consultant), and their children Laura (a college student) and Isobel (a PR manager). All have busy lives and use different kinds of planning systems to keep track of their schedules.

Cecil's job involves a good deal of travel so, along with a Personal Information Manager (PIM) he uses a Personal Digital Assistant (PDA) that includes a calendar, a To-Do list, a telephone and address directory, and a memo pad. It works in tandem with his computer, and the PIM and PDA calendars update each other. His ambition is to have the latest integrated PDA/cell phone device.

Reva feels more comfortable with paper and uses a wall calendar as her planning tool. She works from home and her schedule is fairly simple, so the calendar works well to keep track of her plans, and each family member can keep track of everyone else's schedule at a glance.

Laura prefers a paper-based planner. She has more on her To-Do list than her mother, and her planner is easy to use and always at hand. The downside is that if she loses it, there is no backup, and it can become bulky. When information changes, she has to rewrite entries.

Isobel makes use of a PIM program for planning, and has adapted the electronic planner to emulate the features that she liked best on her paper planner. She uses a notebook when out with clients, and enters new appointments into her personal laptop when she gets home.

Utilize Time and Money

A vital source of leverage comes from other people's time, which allows you to expand the "power" you exert enormously – imagine a senior manager with a big department supporting him. But, time is also money.

Make Use of Other People's Time

We have already looked at delegation within your team, but it is also possible to barter for the skills and time of co-workers or people elsewhere within your organization. This can be an effective approach where funds are limited and where you do not have the right to delegate work. Bartering, however, often takes a lot of effort and people's expectations of recompense can often be unrealistic.

Bringing in outside expertise only when you need it has obvious cost advantages, and by using the skills of experts you achieve quicker and better outcomes. It can be highly cost-effective to hire a consultant for a short, focused exercise, but their time is expensive, so make sure he or she has the expertise you need, and define tasks carefully.

CASE study: Buying in Expertise

Fatima was struggling to launch her home business. Skilled friends had promised to use their expertise to help get her business up and running, but they were slow and projects suffered. Because her relationships with friends had also began to suffer, Fatima decided to use her savings to place properly funded commercial projects with carefully chosen suppliers. She then managed these projects through to conclusion. Soon, blockages were broken and her business was booming.

• *Fatima realized that, because her friends had full-time jobs and were giving her free help in their spare time, they had put her, understandably, at the bottom of their lists of priorities.*
• *By deciding to place the work commercially, Fatima was able to make sure that she got what she wanted – when she wanted it. And because she was employing her suppliers on a professional basis, she was given priority and they were as helpful possible.*

Effective Outsourcing Techniques

HIGH IMPACT	NEGATIVE IMPACT
• Outsourcing complete and clearly defined tasks	• Outsourcing when responsibilities are not clearly defined
• Outsourcing skilled activities that occur infrequently	• Maintaining expensive, infrequently-used, skills in-house
• Outsourcing complex, non-core jobs to expert organizations	• Keeping complex, non-core activities in-house

Outsource Effectively

Many of the principles that we discussed in the context of delegating also apply to outsourcing. In both cases you farm out a non-preferred, low-priority, routine, or specialized task so that you can concentrate on preferred, high-priority, or high-payoff ones. Where your team is over-stretched or not trained in the appropriate area, or where people outside the team are able to do the task efficiently, you should think about outsourcing.

Outsourcing non-core tasks frees time to focus on core operations

Many large organizations work on the basis of carrying out tasks that are a critical part of their mission, while outsourcing necessary, but non-core, jobs. By doing this, they can often get a better job done by a specialist at a lower cost. The classic example of this is outsourcing management of the payroll.

Free Up Personal Time

Outsourcing makes good sense in your personal life, too. You probably have a stack of jobs and projects calling for your attention, preventing you from enjoying weekends relaxing with your family. You spend money to hire the services of plumbers, babysitters, and electricians, so why not hire people like cleaners, shirt-ironers, and gardeners? You can always earn more money, but you can't get time back.

Money – A Fact of Life

The old saw that "money is the root of all evil" is a misquotation: the original saying refers to the *love* of money. Money in itself is morally neutral and can create a great deal of good. However, you need to use it in order to realize its benefits: if you don't pay, you don't get the leverage – that's just the way it is. However, once money is available, people will make tremendous efforts to help you. This is why people say, "you need money to make money". However, there are ways around this.

Keep Your Costs Down

If you have no money, start up a business with a low capital requirement, such as a home-based service business. Start on a small scale and slowly grow in size by reinvesting the money that you make. The business's leverage grows at the same time. Building a good business using internally generated cash can often be slow, but the rewards can be huge.

Borrow Money

You may be in a position to borrow from friends and family, on a very small scale. However, be sure to pay them back, or you'll end up very lonely. On a larger scale, it may be possible to borrow from a bank. In either case, you have

think SMART

Rethink your attitude to money if you want to use it more effectively. Money is not an end in itself; you need to make use of it if you want it to be productive.

By using money intelligently, you can quickly attract the help and resources you need to achieve your goals. But, if you try to hoard it, or are hesitant in your use of it, you will find it much harder to win these resources.

Carry Out a Leverage SWOT Analysis

SWOT stands for **Strengths**, **Weaknesses**, **Opportunities**, and **Threats**. To carry out a leverage SWOT, think through your strengths, the resources you can access, and the types of leverage you could use. Then identify the opportunities that these open up for you with respect to leverage. For example:

→ With your workload under control, you now have the time to realize your dream of setting up that out-of-hours business.
→ If you have some spare cash, you can buy in the skills needed to get your business off to a good start.

Next, look at your weaknesses with respect to leverage, and think about the threats these expose you to. Then act appropriately:

→ If you don't have the skills you need to run your dream business, you risk it failing. Now is the time to book appropriate training.

an obligation to research and plan thoroughly, and you must be confident that you can repay that money. If you can't, you will find it very difficult to raise money in the future. If you use the money that you borrow wisely, your business is likely to be up and running that much more quickly.

"Angels" and Investors

Business angels and venture capital companies can give you massive leverage, but to raise it you must have strong, well-rehearsed business plans and a good team. You also need to be prepared to work extremely hard and grow your business very fast – after all, if you can't achieve the growth you have projected, you stand to lose everything you've worked for. However, if you want to quickly maximize your leverage, and your idea and ambitions justify it, this can be a great way to go.

Index

Picture Credits

Key: (c) = centre, (r) = right, (l) = left, (t) = top, (b) = below, (tl) = top left, (tc) =
top centre, (tr) = top right, (bl) below left, (bc) below centre, (br) = below right.

1 Roger Dixon/DK Images (l), LWA-Stephen Welstead/Corbis (c), LWA- JDC/Corbis
(r); **2:** Anne Rippy/Photonica/Getty; **3** Roger Dixon/DK Images; **4** JBJ Productions/
Zefa/Corbis; **6** Roger Dixon/DK Images; **8** Michael Keller/Corbis (l), Corbis (cl),
Grace/Zefa/Corbis (cr), Corbis (r); **15** WireImageStock/Masterfile; **26** Roger Dixon/
DK Images; **29** Corbis; **31** LWA- JDC/Corbis; **35** Roger Dixon/DK Images;
42 Roger Dixon/DK Images; **49** Royalty-Free/Corbis; **57** Roger Dixon/DK Images;
59 Roger Dixon/DK Images; **61** Roger Dixon/DK Images; **65** Todd Pearson/The
Image Bank/Getty; **70** Roger Dixon/DK Images; **76** Winfred Evers/Photonica/Getty;
84 Roger Dixon/DK Images; **87** Anne Rippy/Photonica/Getty; **89** Roger Dixon/DK
Images; **93** Roger Dixon/DK Images; **99** Corbis; **104** Roger Dixon/DK Images;
107 Popperfoto/Alamy; **109** Stockbyte/Getty; **113** JBJ Productions/Zefa/Corbis (t),
Roger Dixon/DK Images (bl), Shoot/Zefa/Corbis (bc), LWA-Stephen Welstead/
Corbis (br).

Dorling Kindersley would like to thank the following models: Shannon Beatty,
Katie Dock, Caroline D'Souza, Thomas Jaggs, Ken Jones, Tony Limerick,
Traci Salter, Helen Spencer, Ann Thompson.

For further information see www.dkimages.com

Author's Acknowledgments

I would like to thank Namita Anand, for her help and research, Alan Lakein,
inventor of time management, for his comments and wise suggestions, and
Rachel and Alex Manktelow, for just being fantastic.

Author's Biography

JAMES MANKTELOW is CEO of MindTools.com, the Internet's most visited career
skills resource. Prior to Mind Tools, James' career spanned strategic analysis,
business development, marketing, production and project management, business
analysis, and consultancy for major corporations in most European countries. He
has led teams at all corporate levels and has worked with others to build two
successful companies. He is author of *Mind Tools* and *Stress Tools*, and co-author
of *Make Time for Success* and *How to Lead: Discover the Leader Within You*.